MW00528154

Global Initiatives of Ecumenical Patriarch Bartholomew

"This important book is both a gift and a challenge to Christians of all traditions and backgrounds, as well as to others who share with us the stewardship of this planet Earth, 'our island home.' In these pages there is much of value for anyone who would dare to follow Jesus and his Way of Love for all of God's children and all of creation."

—The Most Reverend Michael B. Curry, presiding bishop of the Episcopal Church and author of *Love is the Way*

"It is such a gracious filial duty to celebrate, with this publication, the stalwart figure and the eminently moral voice that His All-Holiness Patriarch Bartholomew is in ecumenical relations, in international policy formulation, and in thinking about care for the earth, our common home. So beautifully do the words of Ben Sirach apply to him: a counsellor in his prudence, a seer of all things in prophecy, and a resolute prince of God's flock (Sirach 44:3–4)."

—Cardinal Peter K. A. Turkson, chancellor of the Pontifical Academy of Sciences and the Pontifical Academy of Social Sciences

"This book holds considerable, perhaps even immeasurable, riches. These are our prophets—prophets of unity, peace, freedom, sustainability, climate justice, and ultimately, prophets of hope—who refuse capitulation either to a false irenicism or to despair. An essential volume!"

—Jennifer Newsome Martin, author of *Hans Urs von Balthasar and the Critical Appropriation of Russian Religious Thought*

"Archdeacon Chryssavgis has had a front-row seat to the remarkable leadership and ministry of His All-Holiness Ecumenical Patriarch Bartholomew. In publishing this compilation of Bartholomew's prophetic and courageous statements, Chryssavgis has done a great service for those who stand in awe of the Ecumenical Patriarch's witness to the power of the gospel and his hope for Christian friendship and unity."

—Rev. Austin I. Collins, C.S.C., vice president for mission engagement and church affairs, University of Notre Dame

"*Global Initiatives of Ecumenical Patriarch Bartholomew* is an invaluable resource for understanding the life and ministry of a most remarkable hierarch. Therefore, in a very real way, Chryssavgis prepares us for an informed reading of the joint (and hence truly ecumenical) groundbreaking documents that follow."

—Joseph M. McShane, S.J., president emeritus of Fordham University

"Ecumenical Patriarch Bartholomew is widely recognized as one of the most significant and influential religious leaders in our time. Those familiar with his writings and addresses will welcome this volume to the library of Patriarch Bartholomew's wisdom, while those new to his thinking and ministry will find this book an excellent introduction to his work."

—Daniel P. Horan, O.F.M., author of *All God's Creatures*

"This important collection reveals Patriarch Bartholomew's consistent and unrelenting concern to connect the Christian faith and Christian moral values with the moral questions that lie behind political choices and challenge governments, churches, and individuals."

—Brian Daley, S.J., author of *God Visible*

Global Initiatives

of

Ecumenical Patriarch Bartholomew

Global Initiatives

of

Ecumenical Patriarch Bartholomew

Peace, Reconciliation, and Care for Creation

Edited by

JOHN CHRYSSAVGIS

Foreword by

JOHN I. JENKINS, C.S.C.

University of Notre Dame Press
Notre Dame, Indiana

Published by University of Notre Dame Press
Notre Dame, Indiana 46556
undpress.nd.edu

Published in the United States of America

Library of Congress Control Number: 2023931105

ISBN: 978-0-268-20558-4 (Hardback)
ISBN: 978-0-268-20560-7 (WebPDF)
ISBN: 978-0-268-20557-7 (Epub)

CONTENTS

F O R E W O R D

John I. Jenkins, C.S.C.

That they all may be one
—John 17:21

In the wake of the historic and pathbreaking meeting between Pope Paul VI and Patriarch Athenagoras in Jerusalem in 1964, Pope Paul VI entrusted a vital ecumenical task to my predecessor as president of Notre Dame, the Reverend Theodore Hesburgh, C.S.C. The Holy Father asked Father Hesburgh to build on the momentum of this meeting by overseeing and stewarding an ecumenical center in Jerusalem, which would serve as a place of meeting and exchange. This initiative would become the Tantur Ecumenical Institute, an oasis of encounter among Christians whose work has continued unabated since its first programs launched in 1972. Through this process, the University of Notre Dame was given the privilege and responsibility of serving the ecumenical endeavor, something we have taken very seriously ever since.

It is against this backdrop of Notre Dame's longstanding aspiration to contribute to the work of Christian unity at the highest levels, and particularly with the Orthodox with whom we share so much, that the inspirational visit to our campus in October 2021 of His All-Holiness Ecumenical Patriarch Bartholomew should be understood. Not, that is, as a standalone event, but as a high point and expression of Notre Dame's ongoing efforts in the realm of Christian cooperation and reconciliation.

The visit of Patriarch Bartholomew, the spiritual leader of 300 million Orthodox Christians worldwide, reinforced and reinvigorated Notre Dame's sense of the importance of respect and collaborative effort across divides in order to deal with the urgent problems of our time. As a great Christian and religious leader, Patriarch Bartholomew does not think in insular terms. In his powerful address given at the conferral of the Doctor of Laws degree at Notre Dame's Basilica of the Sacred Heart (reproduced in full in this volume), he repeatedly emphasized the need for all the dimensions of human life to work together: the intellectual, the political, the scientific, the moral, the spiritual. Without such cooperation, the challenges faced by the world, preeminently including climate change, risk remaining unmet and unsolved. We need, as he puts it, to "always remember the vertical dimension *alongside*—and never at the *expense* of—the horizontal dimension of the social gospel." This is the message of the Cross. Similarly, he tells us, "religion must function and serve in *connection* with—and never in *isolation* from—science."

The leadership role of Patriarch Bartholomew in raising awareness of and addressing the ecological crisis on a global scale can hardly be overstated: his epithet "the Green Patriarch" is fully earned. Several of the joint statements included in this volume demonstrate the breadth and depth of that role over more than three decades of patriarchal ministry. It is especially heartening for us at Notre Dame, where our own approach and priorities as a global Catholic research university very much align with those of the patriarch. In particular, Notre Dame's unique role in bringing together at the highest level the academic and the spiritual, faith and science, aims to embody that holistic understanding of human development and flourishing repeatedly called for by Patriarch Bartholomew and wholly consonant with the highest ideals of Catholic higher education.

I trust the reader will find, as I do, much inspiration in this collection of texts. Whether the issue is climate change, global health (including the COVID-19 pandemic), intra-Christian dialogue, modern slavery, or the contemporary refugee crisis, Patriarch Bartholomew has a way of awakening his listener and reader to empathy but also, and crucially, to action. He is, in that way, not only a spiritual leader, a moral force, but also a global educator of souls. The University of Notre Dame, since the days of our founder, Father Edward Sorin, has consistently aspired to be a "force for good in the world." Meeting with Patriarch Bartholomew, hearing him speak on the urgent issues of our day with such conviction and moral authority, reminded me of that aspiration: a force for good had come into our midst, and was inspiring us to live up to our own ideal of being a force for good in our world. This volume of texts, with an expert introduction to the person and role of Patriarch Bartholomew by Father John Chryssavgis, is meant as a token of Notre Dame's appreciation for the gift of the patriarch's visit. It is also a token, however, of something bigger: of our ongoing shared commitment to addressing the many and diverse global challenges that we face, and that touch all aspects of human life. It is always heartening when we realize that we are not walking this path alone. As we walk alongside the patriarch, in mutual solidarity, we pray that, by the mercy of God and the embrace of Our Lady, Notre Dame, this common path leads us to ever deeper unity, and ultimately to that perfect oneness willed by our common Lord, Jesus Christ.

INTRODUCTION

Portrait of an Ecumenical Patriarch

John Chryssavgis

---

*The Ecumenical Patriarchate, "the great church of Christ,
is a remarkable phenomenon and notion."*
—Patriarch Theodore Balsamon of Antioch
(twelfth-century canonist)

*The Phanar[1] is . . . a concept. It is a symbol of the potential
to transcend destruction, of the possibility for survival
through coexistence. The Phanar is the art of deriving the
highest excellence from the worst circumstances. The Phanar
is the bearer of supreme values: patience, silence, nobility,
the dignity of the past. . . . It is the guardian of the treasure
of our blameless faith and the sacred tradition of the East, as
well as the other sacred traditions of our race; but it is an
active and dynamic guardian. . . . The Phanar is a school.*
—Metropolitan Meliton of Chalcedon
(1913–1989)

*The Ecumenical Patriarchate is an institution that tran-
scends national boundaries. Had this institution not existed,*

then it most certainly should have been conceived. Without the Ecumenical Patriarchate, Orthodoxy would inevitably submit to the dangers of nationalism and triumphalism, to introversion and isolation, and to a repudiation of the contemporary world.

—Metropolitan John of Pergamon

PRELIMINARY REMARKS

This introduction was intended as a lecture at the invitation of the University of Notre Dame to "prepare the way" for the imminent visit of His All-Holiness Ecumenical Patriarch Bartholomew to the university in October 2021 to receive an Honorary Doctorate in Laws on the thirtieth anniversary of his patriarchal tenure. What I hope to achieve here is to suggest a presence, to paint a circumscribed portrait of a patriarch who has served as archbishop of Constantinople for exactly thirty years. I say "circumscribed portrait" because my words primarily focus on his ecumenical vision. For more personal, historical, and theological details, the reader might look at Olivier Clément's *Conversations with Ecumenical Patriarch Bartholomew I* and my official biography of the patriarch, titled *Bartholomew: Apostle and Visionary*, with a foreword by Pope Francis.[2]

However, let me begin on a personal note. I have worked for the Ecumenical Patriarchate in one capacity or another throughout my ministry of thirty-eight years and served with Patriarch Bartholomew for over thirty of those years; I was serving the church in Australia when Bartholomew was elected to the Throne of Constantinople in 1991 at the young age of fifty-one. It has been a special blessing to research and edit his numerous addresses and writings, some of which formed the basis of his book *Encountering the Mystery* and also appeared in the three volumes of his selected works published by Fordham University Press.[3] This unique privilege has been generously granted to me by the past and present archbishops of America, Demetrios and Elpidophoros.

While there are numerous reasons at times—many times, actually—to feel dispirited at developments in the Orthodox Church, it still feels good to belong to the Ecumenical Patriarchate. I continue to be amazed at the breadth of the Phanar and in particular the vision of its current patriarch and how he envisages the ecumenical nature of a church that should be striving for the communion of all God's people as the precious Body of Christ.

My reflections here are by no means an occasion for arrogance; God knows (and we too know, at least when we are honest with ourselves) our sundry weaknesses. In his preface to the Greek Orthodox Archdiocese 2011 *Yearbook,* the patriarch himself recognized this truth: "In looking back at the two decades of our Patriarchal ministry, we behold days of joy but also days of sorrow; days of light but also days of darkness; days of glory but also days of bitterness; days of excitement and optimism but also days of anxiety and disappointment. . . . Yet with the grace of God, we neither lost our footing through pride nor were crushed by pressure."

HISTORICAL CONTEXT AND CONDITIONS

In many ways, the tenure of His All-Holiness mirrors the story of the Ecumenical Patriarchate through the centuries. Sir Steven Runciman (1903–2000) liked to say, "The great achievement of the Patriarchate was that in spite of humiliation and poverty and disdain, the Orthodox Church endured and endures as a great spiritual force." Indeed, we are a church shaped by the suffering of the cross.

Martyrdom is not exceptional, but it is as essential to the Orthodox Church and its spirituality as to the Ecumenical Patriarchate and its story. For Tertullian, "the blood of the martyrs is the seed of the church." "Give blood and receive the Spirit," said the Desert Fathers. The tradition of martyrs from the early church continues without interruption with the "neomartyrs" in the Ottoman era and the "confessors" in Communist Russia. In my humble opinion, the blood of the martyrs is even what preserves us from the persistent temptation to confuse "the things that are Caesar's" and "the things that are God's" or to forget that "we do not have a permanent city here." It is what led to the designation of the Church of Constantinople as "the church of Christ's poor," a phrase coined by Gennadios Scholarios in the fifteenth century to describe the humiliation of the Great Church of Christ in the wake of the fall of Constantinople.

Winston Churchill once quipped, "The further back you look, the farther forward you can see." Byzantium still remains the best-kept secret in the West. But when one visits the Phanar, one finds oneself in an institution founded by Andrew, the "first called" of the apostles and elder brother of Peter. The first bishop of Byzantium was Stachys (38–54), disciple of the apostle Andrew.

Even the exclusive title "Ecumenical Patriarch" dates from as early as the sixth century and was first adopted by Patriarch John IV (582–95), also known as St. John the Faster, in recognition of the wider pastoral responsibility of Constantinople within the federation of Orthodox churches, which Obolensky called "the Byzantine commonwealth."[4] Patriarch Bartholomew is the 269th successor of the apostle Andrew, the 270th head of his church (as Francis is the 266th pope of Rome). We are speaking of a considerable history and consequential heritage like very few others.

The Ecumenical Patriarchate itself has a history spanning seventeen centuries, during which it retained its administrative offices in the same city, Constantinople/Istanbul. And of course, the entire region is filled with significance for Christendom. All the earliest councils that defined and shaped Christian doctrine were held not in Italy or Greece but in Asia Minor. It is there that St. John (the apostle of love) wrote his Gospel; and it is there that St. Paul (apostle to the nations) visited the earliest communities. "More than any museum or library can ever preserve, the Ecumenical Patriarchate is the eloquent expression of the early church and the living spirit of Byzantium."[5]

Any visitor to Turkey today will witness and wonder at the country's many historical treasures. Among them are the fourth-century walls of Constantine and Theodosius (the surviving ramparts of a magnificent civilization), the fourth-century Church of the Holy Peace (Hagia Irene, where the Creed was completed), the fifth-century Monastery of St. John (where icons were defended and monasticism was reformed by Theodore the Studite in the eighth century), the sixth-century Church of the Holy Wisdom (Hagia Sophia, one of the architectural wonders of the world that radiates the beauty of Orthodox theology and spirituality), the eleventh-century Chora Monastery (which contains extraordinary fourteenth-century frescoes and mosaics), the twelfth-century Pammakaristos Church overlooking the Golden Horn (whose icon of the Mother of God graces the patriarchal church today), and the remarkable cave churches in Cappadocia (where monasticism thrived during the early Christian and Byzantine periods).

Moreover, like the ancient patriarchates of Alexandria, Antioch, and Jerusalem (and even Rome), Constantinople today precariously exists within a political authority, the modern Turkish Republic. Ecumenical Patriarch Bartholomew, however, has been adept at turning difficult challenges from the state into positives. For example, in response to a state decree of 1923 that candidates for election to the Patriarchal Throne "must be Turkish nationals and holders of religious positions within Turkey at the time of the election," Bartholomew persuaded the Turkish government in 2010 to facilitate Turkish citizenship to any and all applicants—thereby expanding the pool of candidates for election. And in response to the forced closure of the Theological School of Halki in 1971, Bartholomew celebrated the school's 150th anniversary in 1994, had President Barack Obama urge its reopening before the Turkish Parliament in 2009, and continues to advocate for his right to train clergy in the ecumenical spirit of his church.

He has restored some 130 churches, chapels, cemeteries, dioceses, centers, monasteries (for men and women), pilgrimages, and institutions in Istanbul and Turkey, as well as the Patriarchal Treasury (of vessels and vestments), the Patriarchal Library (with manuscripts and icons), the Patriarchal Church of St. George, and the Monastery of the Holy Trinity at Halki.[6] In what before his tenure would have been considered inconceivable and impossible, he has celebrated (albeit usually once a year per church) the divine liturgy and feast days in previously closed churches of Asia Minor (forbidden since 1922) in Cappadocia (where he continues to lead annual pilgrimages), Pergamon (one of the churches of the Apocalypse), Myra (the eighth-century church dedicated to St. Nicholas), and Panagia Soumela Monastery (founded in the fourth century).

The latest challenge by the state, of course, is the 2020 conversion into mosques of the Monastery of Christ at Chora and the Hagia Sophia Cathedral, built in the sixth century and the largest domed building in the world for a thousand years before the construction of St. Peter's in Rome. Both the cathedral and the monastery have been museums since 1958 and 1935, respectively, and are recognized as World Heritage Sites by UNESCO, which will be reviewing the conversions. The patriarch, along with the rest of the Christian world, has condemned the conversions and awaits the UNESCO findings.

Move out of Istanbul? It has never crossed his mind. The patriarchate has not left that city in seventeen centuries, except for a brief, fifty-seven-year period in the thirteenth century, when the city was occupied by the Latins and the patriarch took temporary refuge in Nicaea. Bartholomew is definitely not "the last Patriarch in Turkey," to use CNN's sensationalized phrase; he is the one who ensured he will not be the last.

The Throne of Constantinople has been occupied by an extraordinary range of churchmen: saintly theologians, great administrators, and many scarcely remembered figures who had little choice but merely to preserve their ancient office as best they could, usually in dire conditions, for future generations. However, over seventeen centuries only nine patriarchs have completed twenty years of continuous ministry. The history of the Ecumenical Patriarchate is replete with examples of patriarchs serving for just a few years. In the seventeenth century alone, there were fifty-two separate enthronements (for twenty-eight patriarchs), with the Throne vacant for just over a decade. While we think of Patriarch Gregory V's martyrdom as an exception, he is really quite typical of many patriarchs who were tortured, exiled, or executed. Therefore, it is historic that Bartholomew is the longest-serving patriarch in the life of the Ecumenical Patriarchate, the only patriarch since the third century to serve for thirty years. October 22—just days before his visit to Notre Dame—marked the thirtieth anniversary since his election.

ECUMENICAL HEART OF A PATRIARCH

For the Ecumenical Patriarch, the concept of ecumenicity incarnated by the Church of Constantinople "is more than a name;

it is a worldview, a way of life"[7]—not a symbol of triumph or power. The Ecumenical Patriarchate—and, by extension, the Orthodox Church—can play a major role in the contemporary world but only when it becomes the prophetic conscience of the peoples entrusted to it, which will invariably mean divesting itself of the idolatry of *ethnocentrism*—whether Greek or American, Antiochian or Serbian, Russian or Ukrainian—and instead embracing an *ecumenical* Orthodoxy. It must therefore first free itself of provincial arrogance or parochial competitiveness if it is to become a witness to God's healing grace in a divided world.

Below I indicate ways in which the Ecumenical Patriarchate has realized this ecumenical dimension—what Bartholomew himself, in a lecture of 1986, labeled the "ecumenical conscience" and "ecumenical concern" of the church[8]—with a brief look at his relations with other faiths and more extensively with the Catholic Church. This includes some personal and anecdotal aspects of an extraordinary leader and his ministry that indicate his exceptional qualities and illustrate his conception of the church as ecumenical. Here, then, are some of the contours of the patriarch's "ecumenical" breadth and vision over the past thirty years as they are revealed in some of the lesser-known accomplishments of his tenure.

A church stagnated in the past is no more than a precious relic. To remain relevant, the Ecumenical Patriarchate has had to look both ways, like the classical god Janus: while rooted in the historical past, it must remain focused on the tangible present in the spiritual light of the future. And it is this dual nature, or triptych identity, that permits the patriarchate to speak and act boldly about critical contemporary challenges, including reorganizing existing structures within the Orthodox Church itself to be more ecumenical.

Toward an Ecumenical Orthodox Church

At the Patriarchate

The Hierarchs of the Throne
Ecumenical Patriarch Bartholomew was the first to convene assemblies of hierarchs of the Ecumenical Throne, that is, those churches throughout the world that are under the patriarchate's immediate jurisdiction. The assemblies, which began in 1992, only months after his election, were usually biannual gatherings held in Istanbul.

The Holy and Sacred Synod
His All-Holiness decentralized the administrative authority of the church in 2004 by introducing *six* (of a total of twelve) hierarchs from outside Turkey to the Holy and Sacred Synod, the highest decision-making body of the patriarchate. Previously known as the *endemousa*—denoting that the bishops either permanently dwelled in or were passing through Constantinople—this synod was historically (from at least the mid-fifth century) the most powerful decision-making body of the Byzantine Church.

In recent years, it had been reduced solely to the Phanariote bishops,[9] whose tenure was without term limits and whose replacement occurred postmortem. The term limit of the new synodal system is one (ecclesiastical) year (September to August). In 2013 the patriarch further expanded this decentralized synod to include a total of *eleven* bishops from abroad among the twelve synod members. Thus, for instance, in 2014, among the twelve bishops serving on the synod, there were bishops from Chicago, Boston, Toronto, and Mexico. This was a radical change in a millennial-old system and tradition; and there were many who reacted, even resisted.

Canonization of Saints

Over the past thirty years, there have been more than thirty-five Synodal Acts recognizing over 250 new saints on the Orthodox calendar (including a cluster of 150 martyrs at Daou Penteli and an unknown number of martyrs at Naoussa) from Greece, Russia, and Asia Minor but also Western Europe.[10] These include popular contemporary figures, such as Mother Maria Skobt-sova of Paris (2004), Paisios of Mt. Athos (2015), and Sophrony of Essex (2019).

With Other Autocephalous Orthodox Churches

Synaxis of Primates

Ecumenical Patriarch Bartholomew was the first to convene a series of assemblies of the heads of all fourteen autocephalous Orthodox churches. The first was held in Istanbul (1992) just weeks after his election, the most recent in Geneva (2016) in preparation for the Holy and Great Council.

It may seem like a small endeavor, but these prelates had not met since 1872—ironically, at a council held in Constantinople to condemn the heresy of phyletism (ecclesiastical nationalism). Since then, ethnic division and competition precluded any tangible unity or genuine conciliarity—what Leo the Great described at the Fourth Ecumenical Council in Chalcedon (451) as "the incontestable agreement of the entire college of brothers."[11] It was the establishment of national Orthodox churches during the nineteenth century that contributed to a subversion by some of the authority of the Ecumenical Patriarchate. In 1978 the late Fr. John Meyendorff wrote:

> It is unquestionable that the Orthodox conception of the Church recognizes the need for a leadership of the world episcopate, for a certain spokesmanship by the first patriarch, for a ministry of coordination without which concili-

arity is impossible. . . . In the present chaotic years, the Orthodox Church could indeed use wise, objective and authoritative leadership from the ecumenical patriarchate.[12]

The patriarch himself echoed the same sentiments at the Fifth Synaxis of the Heads of Orthodox Churches in Istanbul (2008), when he boldly addressed the primates of the Orthodox Church:

> We have received and preserve the true faith. . . . We commune of the same Body and Blood of our Lord. . . . We basically keep the same liturgical *typikon* and are governed by the same Sacred Canons. Despite this, we must admit in all honesty that sometimes we present an image of incomplete unity, as if we were not one Church, but rather a confederation or a federation of churches. . . . Yet, while the original system of authority emanated from respect for the apostolicity and particularity of the traditions of these ancient Patriarchates, the autocephaly of later Churches grew out of respect for the cultural identity of nations. . . . So we have reached the perception that Orthodoxy comprises a federation of national Churches[,] . . . which somewhat recalls the situation in Corinth when the first letter to the Corinthians was written, the apostle Paul would ask: Is Orthodoxy divided? . . . When we lack a unified voice on contemporary issues and . . . fail to constitute a single Orthodox Church in the so-called Diaspora . . . how can we avoid the image of division in Orthodoxy? . . . As a result, autocephaly becomes a factor of division rather than unity for the Orthodox Church.[13]

Assemblies of Bishops

On the local level, this momentous 2008 address by His All-Holiness inspired the creation of regional Assemblies of Bishops throughout the world, which were established in accordance with a decision of the Pan-Orthodox Pre-Conciliar Conference held in Geneva (2009) to overcome the canonical anomalies of the Orthodox churches in the Diaspora and present a unified witness to the pastoral needs of the faithful.

The principal goal of the Assembly of Canonical Orthodox Bishops of the United States of America is to promote and achieve unity in America by organizing the church according to the ecclesiological and canonical tradition of the Orthodox Church, which requires, for example, that there be only one bishop per diocese. This means that there would be a far more united church in America, and some bishops might be obliged to relinquish their positions. I think one can readily appreciate the challenges involved in this endeavor, and the patriarch is to be commended for his bold promotion of this canonical goal.

The Holy and Great Council
It was as a result of the above-mentioned state within the Orthodox Church that the patriarch urged the prelates to resume and advance preparations for the Holy and Great Council of the Orthodox Church.

Conversations about a Great Council began almost one hundred years ago, but Ecumenical Patriarch Athenagoras held the first of a series of Pan-Orthodox Consultations and Pre-Conciliar Conferences (in Rhodes and Geneva) in 1961, a year before Vatican II. At the invitation of Ecumenical Patriarch Bartholomew, the Fourth Pre-Conciliar Pan-Orthodox Conference met at the Orthodox Center of the Ecumenical Patriarchate in Chambésy, Geneva, in June 2009. The goal was, as Patriarch Bartholomew said in 2008, "to practice what we preach about unity."

The vision of the patriarch—at least in my humble opinion—was ultimately to bring about sufficiently proper conditions of unity to convene the Holy and Great Council of the Orthodox Church, which he ultimately convened in June 2016 in Crete. Since the first day of his enthronement—arguably from before his election and enthronement—His All-Holiness has systematically and patiently worked assiduously and advanced steadily toward the convocation of this Great Council, which in some respects was the first in many centuries, possibly since the Seventh Ecumenical Council in 787. Never before was such an extensive assembly of bishops convened. In the past, there were only five patriarchates to contend with, and these were controlled by a powerful emperor. It would not be far-fetched to claim that the Great Council—with all its flaws and absences—would have been inconceivable in the previous two millennia.

Critics sometimes sarcastically label our process disorganized. It is, however, somewhat naive to dismiss disputes among various churches as resulting merely from rivalries of power. Such a perception is not entirely inaccurate, and it is often very frustrating to those inside and outside our church. But it is arguably a more democratic, conciliar method than what occurs in other churches—whether in the hierarchical structure of the papacy or in the horizontal system of Protestantism. Still, the Orthodox churches frequently exploit the notion of consensus, inevitably manipulating it to create obfuscation or obstruction.

Toward an Ecumenical Christianity

The inter-Christian service of His All-Holiness probably attracts the greatest amount of criticism and slander from his fellow Orthodox. Yet the world is fortunate to have in our patriarch a pastor of great wisdom, capable of holding the diverse problems of our day firmly within the generous bounds of Orthodoxy. Christians of all confessions recognize his ecumenical charity and courage.

Far ahead of his time—and far ahead of his peers—Patriarch Bartholomew has forged new ground in this area. The ecumenical openness of the Church of Constantinople is literally a harbinger of fresh air. It is much harder for the ignorance and intolerance of some metropolitans in Greece or Cyprus, but also in Russia or Serbia, for instance, ever to be nurtured within our patriarchate, where there is a marked and prolonged history of inter-Christian relations, ecumenical openness, and theological dialogue throughout the centuries but especially in more recent decades.

It was Ecumenical Patriarch Joachim III (1878–84, 1901–12) who issued the historic encyclical in 1902 addressing the importance of relations among Orthodox, Roman Catholic, and Protestant Christians. In 1920 the Holy Synod of the Ecumenical Patriarchate issued the groundbreaking encyclical "To the Churches of Christ Everywhere," which proposed a "League of Churches" and declared that the Orthodox Church "holds that rapprochement between the various Christian Churches and fellowship between them is not excluded by the doctrinal differences which exist between them."

Toward an Ecumenical Coexistence with Islam

Patriarch Bartholomew has cultivated relationships with Islamic countries. Because Orthodox Christianity has a 550-year history of coexistence with Islam, His All-Holiness traveled to Palestine, Libya, Syria, Egypt, Iran, Jordan, Azerbaijan, Qatar, Kazakhstan, and Bahrain, creating more bridges between the two religions than any other Christian leader. Moreover, underlining the fundamental compatibility of Orthodoxy and human rights, religious freedom and democracy, he preaches that violence in the name of religion is a crime against religion. At Ground Zero in New York City in March 2002, he said, "On this planet created by God for us all, there is room for us all."

But let me summarize his interfaith commitment with a personal anecdote. I recall as though it was yesterday the Great Blessing of the Waters on January 6, 2011, the Feast of Epiphany. The patriarch has commemorated the Baptism of Christ in the

Jordan River with a special service on the banks of Istanbul's Golden Horn since 2003. As usual, the Christian commencement of services coincided with the Islamic call to prayer. For some reason, however, the more solemn the Orthodox celebration, the louder the Muslim recording of the call to prayer seems to echo above the Phanar. On this occasion, as the patriarch was about to cast the cross into the waters of the Bosphorus, the recording was disproportionately dissonant and deafening. The patriarch graciously gestured for the service to pause and solemnly bowed his head in prayer, until the *adhan* concluded, whereupon he began singing the hymn of the day and hurled the cross into the river.

Toward an Ecumenical Unity with Rome

The encounters and dialogues either intensified or initiated by Ecumenical Patriarch Bartholomew with a number of Christian confessions is truly extraordinary and exemplary, including churches such as the Anglican Communion and the World Lutheran Federation, as well as ecumenical organizations such as the World Council of Churches and the Conference of European Churches. However, for the remainder of this introduction, I would like to focus on the relations between our two sister churches—Roman Catholic and Orthodox—in their effort to move beyond the schism dating to the eleventh century.

Solemn Events of Reconciliation

Relations between the two sister churches were consolidated with the joint pilgrimage to Jerusalem by Bartholomew and Francis in 2014 to mark the fiftieth anniversary of the meeting in the Holy Land by their predecessors Athenagoras and Paul VI. Those visionary prelates had broken a long silence that spanned ten centuries and culminated in 1965 with the mutual lifting of the anathemas that had divided the Western and Eastern churches since 1054. For me, the most dramatic scene of this apostolic visit in 2014 was the moment when the patriarch assisted the pope (who the previous day had injured his foot) down the steps leading to the stone of the Holy Sepulcher, where they both fell to their knees—a striking image of authority-in-frailty.

Official theological dialogue between our two churches had begun in 1984 but came to a grinding halt over the prickly topic of Uniatism (first in Balamand, Lebanon, in 1993 and then again in Baltimore, Maryland, in 2000). Bartholomew and Benedict XVI renewed their commitment to resume this dialogue, which has subsequently faltered over the critical issue of primacy and conciliarity.

But there has also been a spectacular return of relics. When Patriarch Bartholomew visited Rome in June 2004, Pope John Paul II apologized once again for the Fourth Crusade and the sacking of Constantinople.[14] In response, the patriarch asked not for material compensation but for a return of the relics of Gregory the Theologian and John Chrysostom, his predecessors in Constantinople. It was moving to see these relics deservedly resting on the Patriarchal Throne. This was a radical step toward restoration and reconciliation.

A few years later, on March 19, 2013, the patriarch decided to attend the inaugural mass of Pope Francis in St. Peter's Square. His spontaneous gesture signaled another first: the first time that any leader of either church had ever participated in such a solemn event. It was another piece of an ecumenical puzzle enriching and completing the commitment to dialogue planted in the hearts of these two leaders and reflecting the aspiration of their trailblazing if sometimes controversial forerunners.

Ecumenical and Ecological Commitment

For his pioneering and prolific ecological initiatives, which date to before he was elected ecumenical patriarch, Bartholomew has been named "champion of the earth" by the United Nations Environment Programme (2005), "one of the world's most influential people" by *Time* magazine (2008), "someone who can save the planet" by *The Guardian* (2008), and "the green patriarch" by the international media. He has staked a clear moral and spiritual authority in this area.

Among the unique environmental experiences I count as blessings—while either accompanying or representing His All-Holiness—is attending the formal publication of the "green" encyclical *Laudato Si'*, released by Pope Francis in Rome on the morning of June 18, 2015, in the new synod hall of the Paul VI building at the Vatican. While the papal letter was long awaited and historic in many ways, this was the first time that a papal encyclical referred at all, let alone so prominently, to an Orthodox prelate—in this case, the ecumenical patriarch. It was also the first time that a non-Catholic—in this case, an Orthodox hierarch[15]—was invited to launch the encyclical jointly with the director of the relevant pontifical office.

Thus, in the opening pages of the document—after mention of his immediate predecessors—Pope Francis penned three paragraphs under the subhead, "United by the same concern" (paragraphs 7–9). The *New York Times* reported on June 18, 2015, "Francis tapped a wide variety of sources in his encyclical, partly to underscore the universality of his message. He cite[d] passages from his two papal predecessors, John Paul II and Benedict XVI, and [drew] prominently from a religious ally, Patriarch Bartholomew I of Constantinople, leader of the Eastern Orthodox Church."

Pope Francis was from the outset aware of the ecumenical foundations and implications of his encyclical, even plainly stating that he "shares the hope of full communion" with the ecumenical patriarch (paragraph 7). In this context, communications between the Phanar and the Vatican throughout the lengthy drafting process of the anticipated encyclical demonstrated yet another aspect of ecumenical encounter and openness in the search for common ground and mutual witness. In this case, the dialogue was grounded in a personal and paramount friendship between a pope and a patriarch. This book includes a number of significant joint statements between Patriarch Bartholomew and Pope Francis.

Ecumenical Dialogue with Global Implications

Both Pope Francis and Patriarch Bartholomew have repeatedly reminded us that concern for creation and compassion for people are inseparable, like two sides of the same coin. The intimate connection between sustainability of nature and solidarity with neighbor was evident when, one year after the publication of *Laudato Si'*, the pope and the patriarch visited Greece at the invitation of Archbishop Ieronymos of Athens on April 16, 2016. Once again the world observed an ecumenical commitment to social justice, as well as the responsibility and priority of the church in the contemporary world.

Theological dialogues and ecumenical relations are of paramount importance, but they are often carried out to *gain* something (whether greater clarity, fuller unity, or even—sadly—more converts). By contrast, the visit to the island of Lesvos aimed at *giving* something: namely, hope to the hundreds of detainees and desperate refugees from the Middle East and northern Africa. For the pope and the patriarch, coming face-to-face with refugees from northern Africa and the Middle East indicated a practical and pastoral response by the churches of East and West to a tragic crisis in our world. It also marked a compelling reassessment of ecumenical relations at a time when the world is abandoning victims of religious extremism and persecution or deciding their fate on exclusively financial terms and national interests.

The power of ecumenism lies in beginning to open up beyond ourselves and our own, our communities and our churches.

It brings divided Christians before a common task that they must face together. It is giving priority to solidarity and service. This brings me to my final point about the global implications of ecumenical dialogue. What becomes immediately apparent in *Laudato Si'* is the emphasis on the socioeconomic dimensions of climate justice. The ecological crisis is not simply about what people have done to God's creation but also—and especially—about the societal nexus that surrounds the natural world. This broader aspect of our response to global warming is the focus of two corresponding and consequential documents that appeared independently around the same time—indeed both of them during the novel coronavirus pandemic—at the Vatican and the Phanar.

Fratelli Tutti was announced by Pope Francis in September 2020 and released on the Feast of St. Francis of Assisi in October 2020.[16] *For the Life of the World* was endorsed by the Holy Synod of the Ecumenical Patriarchate in January 2020 and published during Great Lent in March 2020.[17] *Fratelli Tutti* calls for greater fraternity and social connection; *For the Life of the World* calls for greater awareness of and engagement in social responsibility. The Catholic encyclical was the third issued by the current pope, while the Orthodox document was the first commissioned by the Ecumenical Patriarchate on "the social ethos of the Orthodox Church."[18]

The process of the patriarchal document was both extraordinary and exceptional.[19] A special commission was appointed by the ecumenical patriarch in 2017; responses to regional social challenges were submitted by dioceses in the jurisdiction of the Ecumenical Patriarchate throughout the world in 2018; drafts of the document were circulated and critiqued by clergy (from bishops through monastics) and laity (theologians and historians); and the text was formally submitted in 2019 to the Ecumenical Patriarchate, whereupon a special subcommittee was appointed, and the Holy Synod formally approved the document for publication in early 2020. After a final review by Metropolitan

John (Zizioulas) of Pergamon and Metropolitan Kallistos (Ware) of Diokleia, the document appeared in over fifteen languages during Lent 2020.[20]

This is why it came as no surprise when the ecumenical patriarch drew parallels between the two documents in his formal address to the papal delegation at the Phanar on the occasion of the Feast of St. Andrew (November 30, 2020):

> The recent Encyclical *Fratelli Tutti* of His Holiness Pope Francis exceptionally proves the multidimensional interest of the Church of Rome in the vast social questions. In the same vein, three years ago we commissioned a group of esteemed Orthodox theologians, assigning to them the responsibility of drafting a document—based on decisions of the Holy and Great Council, while grounded on theological principles of our tradition—about the social ethos of the Orthodox Church. This document . . . entitled *For the Life of the World: The Social Ethos of the Orthodox Church*, has already provoked fruitful conversation.

Today the document is part and parcel of statements released by the Phanar. It was even cited in the ecumenical patriarch's address at the convocation held in his honor by the University of Notre Dame.

It is hardly coincidental but quite providential that these two bishops lead their respective churches at this critical moment. This may well be why they also face so much criticism in religious and secular circles alike. This is the case when it comes to their ecological conviction; it is certainly the case when it comes to their ecumenical commitment. What the two leaders have succeeded in doing—in their own way, within their own communion—is to demonstrate how ecumenical dialogue is essential to the Christian mandate. It is not something superficial or supererogatory to our vocation as Christians. It is profoundly central to our doctrinal and spiritual identity.

Religion may not always transform people, but it can certainly mobilize them. This will not be achieved by politics, which will inevitably divide people; even culture can sometimes prove divisive. Religion, however, can have a huge influence and impact.

CONCLUDING REMARKS

Ecumenical Patriarch Bartholomew has brought the Orthodox Church to the forefront of international attention. He has addressed such media venues as *60 Minutes*, as well as numerous think tanks and academic institutions, the World Economic Forum in Davos, the World Bank, the White House, the United Nations, and the European Parliament, among others. At the personal invitation of Pope Benedict, he addressed the Roman Catholic Synod of Bishops in the Sistine Chapel (2008); Bartholomew is the only Orthodox patriarch ever to do so.

Yet very few people could have foreseen in 1991 that Ecumenical Patriarch Bartholomew would become one of the world's most renowned and respected religious figures. What the patriarch has achieved is nothing less than miraculous. By addressing problems of wider importance, he has reinvested his ancient office with a moral authority and public profile of which many religious leaders can only dream. In the testimonial of the former archbishop of Canterbury, Rowan Williams, "Bartholomew has turned the relative political weakness of his office into a strength."

This strength-in-weakness and leadership-in-service is precisely how the Orthodox Church will meet the challenge of unity today. When all the historical structures (like bishops and councils) and essential features (like liturgy and spirituality) are placed at the service of God and the Gospel, when the nefarious ambitions for primacy no longer create centers of power but places of communion, and when the rediscovery of a more ecumenical perspective of the church addresses the people of God as the precious Body of Christ, then I believe that little by little we can break down the boundaries of division and bear witness instead to reconciliation in a world that increasingly aches for hope and healing.

CLIMATE CHANGE

An Ecumenical Imperative

Ecumenical Patriarch Bartholomew

It is a unique privilege to stand before this assembly of university staff and students, as well as visitors from the region and all over the United States, to receive the preeminent honorary award of Doctor of Laws from the University of Notre Dame for the initiatives of the Ecumenical Patriarchate in response to the foremost challenge of our time, climate change.

We are especially honored that such a commendation comes from an academic institution with demonstrated climate and energy research, with sustained environmental and social programs, and with passionate student involvement and commitment. All of these have resulted in a comprehensive plan by the school's administration to reduce your school's carbon footprint by half within the present decade. Even the overarching theme of your scholastic year is focused on the global climate

This address was delivered during the convocation for the bestowing of an Honorary Doctorate in Laws on Ecumenical Patriarch Bartholomew by the University of Notre Dame on October 30, 2021.

crisis. We therefore take pride in congratulating you on these admirable efforts.

However, this convocation occurs in the context of yet another global challenge. Both climate change and the coronavirus pandemic are rightly labeled crises. You may be aware that the etymological root of *crisis* (κρίσις) is a Greek word that signifies "judgment." The truth is that we are all judged by our response to or rejection of defining moments in our lives. Ironically, the strategies used to dismiss climate change and COVID-19 adhere to a similar pattern and are adopted by the same people.

Both climate and COVID therefore present us with an unprecedented problem but at the same time an unparalleled opportunity. This is why, throughout the world, we witnessed how the pandemic revealed the very *best* in human nature, as well as the very *worst* in human indifference. We observed how first responders were willing to sacrifice their lives for the sake of caring for and healing others. Yet we also noticed how some institutions and individuals stubbornly insisted on sustaining profits over people while persistently championing their own rights over the safety of others.

This is precisely where the role of the church becomes paramount, because a Christian should always remember the vertical dimension *alongside*—and never at the *expense* of—the horizontal dimension of the social gospel. It is of course always difficult to maintain a delicate balance between these two dimensions, but that is the message of the Cross, which marks the tension and intersection between the earthly and the heavenly.

In this respect, it is an important but humbling lesson that the church has learned during this time: namely, that religion must function and serve in *connection* with—and never in *isolation* from—science. The challenges of our time will not be overcome without faith; but faith alone will certainly not overcome the problems of our time. Research and medicine are gifts from

God; they supply answers to the question, "How?" Faith and theology are also gifts from God; they provide responses to the question, "Why?"

The ultimate struggle for Christians is how we can translate the doctrine of the Holy Trinity as communion and the teaching about humankind created in the image of God into the daily and practical life of the world. In other words, how can the kingdom of heaven be reflected in the reality of earth? What does liturgy look like when it is extended to the service of the world? In the seventh century, St. Maximus the Confessor spoke of a "cosmic liturgy." This broader worldview is what enables us to imagine a world that is different from the one we have created or become accustomed to. It is the conviction that something which has not yet happened *can actually happen* with the cooperation of everyone and the synergy of God. It is, as the Letter to the Hebrews says, "the substance of things hoped for and the evidence of things not seen" (Heb 11.1).

Like climate change, then, the global crisis of the novel coronavirus has presented us with ultimate questions about life and death, sickness and suffering, as well as healthcare and justice. And what we are facing cannot naively be dismissed as a temptation or a trial. It is not some kind of punishment from God or threat from government. And it is certainly not a result of "sin" or a revelation of the "end."

In fact, our response to COVID-19 is the very arena where all Christian believers—and, indeed, all people of goodwill—are called to be and struggle. Otherwise, the truth is that we are not living up to our vocation as preachers of Christ crucified (1 Cor 1.23) and disciples of our Lord who was buried and arose on the third day (1 Cor 15.4).

Similarly, protecting the natural environment is neither a liberal nor a sentimental response. It involves constant pain and forgiveness, unrelenting preference and priority for what we truly value, for what really matters. It is the spiritual and moral response, whereby we become a healing and transformative presence among our neighbors and on our planet.

This brings us to another critical dimension of climate change and COVID-19. It is what we call *the ecumenical imperative* of our response. We faith leaders are called humbly and patiently to cooperate with leaders in the scientific and academic worlds, as well as the corporate and political domains. This interconnectedness reminds us that the earth unites us beyond any doctrinal, social, or cultural differences. The power of ecumenical dialogue lies in opening up beyond ourselves and our own interests, beyond our confessions or religions. It means learning to speak the language of care and compassion. And creation care brings us divided, insulated believers before a common task that we must face together.

As you know, we recently issued a statement with our brothers Pope Francis of Rome and Archbishop Justin of Canterbury. It was the first time that the three of us have jointly signed an appeal on the urgency of ecological integrity and sustainability. In our statement, "we called on everyone to listen to the cry of the earth and to the cry of people living with poverty, examining their behavior and pledging meaningful sacrifices for the sake of the earth which God has given us."

Dear friends, it is our obligation before God, neighbor, and creation to assume responsibility for addressing climate change and suppressing the pandemic. After the historic Holy and Great Council held in Crete five years ago, in the wake of long preparations that lasted an entire century, the Ecumenical Patriarchate appointed an official commission to draft a document on the social implications of our faith. This text, which is titled *For the Life of the World: Toward a Social Ethos of the Orthodox Church* and was endorsed by our Holy and Sacred Synod, reminds us that "we are dependent creatures, creatures ever in communion, and hence we are also morally responsible not only for ourselves or for those whom we immediately influence or affect, but for the whole of the created order."[1]

So when, some twenty-five years ago (in Santa Barbara, California, 1997), we defined abusing the natural environment as sin, we were pleading with people to revise their conception of what is right and what is wrong. As human beings, we surely understand that we cannot hurt our brothers and sisters, that there are consequences to our actions—moral, social, and legal. Why then do we not grasp the fact that there should be repercussions—moral, social, and legal—when we harm God's creation? This is why we applaud efforts to expand relevant statutes of international law to include ecocide defined as the unlimited and unlawful destruction of ecosystems through oil drilling spills, industrial fishing and livestock farming, plastic pollution, and mountaintop removal, but also nuclear weapons and testing? In the same framework, we also welcome the discussion in the Latin code of Canon Law to include a provision calling every believer not only to avoid damaging creation as our common home, but also to enhance the natural environment. All of this certainly echoes the Orthodox worldview that considers both ecology and canon law as a process of applied ecclesiology or a journey of spirituality in practice.

And on this journey, it is *you*—college students—who offer us the optimism that we yearn: the readiness to accept change and sacrifice, the capacity to overcome polarization and partisanship, and the conviction to be catalysts of social and ecological justice, as well as the opportunity to save democracy and our planet. May God grant your generation the necessary wisdom and courage to continue leading this charge and mandate.

Joint Statements

As part of the "dialogue of love" initiated by Ecumenical Patriarch Athenagoras and Pope Paul VI in the mid-1960s, an exchange of formal visits by respective delegations would travel to the Vatican and the Phanar to attend the patronal feasts[1] of the two sister churches on June 29 and November 30.[2] On June 29, 1995, Ecumenical Patriarch Bartholomew broke with the custom of commissioning a formal delegation and personally attended the patronal celebrations of Pope John Paul II in St. Peter's Basilica.[3]

The first example of a statement signed simultaneously—in fact, this was a matter of a common gesture in two separate statements on the same issue but not signed jointly—by an ecumenical patriarch and a pope pertained to the "lifting of anathemas" between Constantinople and Rome on December 7, 1965.[4]

To my knowledge, the first jointly signed statement between an ecumenical patriarch and a pope was issued by Paul VI and Athenagoras on October 28, 1967. This "common declaration" expressed joy at the rediscovery of the two sister churches and hope that they might jointly address "pastoral, social, and spiritual" challenges in order to "promote justice and peace throughout the world."[5]

1

A second statement was signed jointly on November 30, 1979, by Ecumenical Patriarch Demetrios and Pope John Paul II "to announce that the Theological Dialogue [between the Orthodox and Roman Catholic Churches was] about to begin and to make public the list of the members of the Joint Orthodox-Catholic Commission" that officially opened what became known as the "dialogue of truth" on May 29, 1980, which complemented the "dialogue of love."[6]

This powerful symbolic gesture of jointly initiating, crafting, and signing common statements was reinforced and amplified by Ecumenical Patriarch Bartholomew in the early years of his tenure as archbishop of Constantinople–New Rome. Bartholomew has to date initiated and issued ten joint statements or declarations with various popes on diverse issues during his thirty-year patriarchal ministry.

These statements are assembled and published here for the first time, one of them also signed by Archbishop Justin Welby of Canterbury. They are supplemented by two statements (one on climate change and health, the other on human trafficking and modern slavery) signed by Patriarch Bartholomew and Archbishop Welby.

— 1 —

On the Importance of Dialogue

Pope John Paul II and
Ecumenical Patriarch Bartholomew

THE VATICAN, JUNE 29, 1995

Blessed be the God and Father of our Lord
Jesus Christ, who has blessed us in Christ with
every spiritual blessing.
                                        —Ephesians 1.3

On the evening of Thursday, June 29, Pope John Paul II and Ecumenical Patriarch Bartholomew signed a Common Declaration at the Vatican prior to the patriarch's departure. This is a translation of the Declaration, which was originally crafted in Italian.

1. We thank God for this brotherly meeting of ours which took place in His name and with the firm intention of obeying His will that His disciples be one (Jn 17.21). Our meeting has followed other important events which have seen our Churches declare their desire to relegate the excommunications of the past to oblivion and to set out on the way to reestablishing full communion. Our venerable predecessors, Athenagoras I and Paul VI, became pilgrims to Jerusalem in order to meet in the Lord's name, precisely where the Lord, by His Death and Resurrection, brought humanity forgiveness and salvation. Subsequently, their meetings at the Phanar and in Rome have initiated this new tradition of fraternal visits in order to foster a true dialogue of charity and truth. This exchange of visits was repeated during the ministry of Patriarch Demetrios, when, among other things, the theological dialogue was formally opened. Our newfound brotherhood in the name of the one Lord has led us to frank discussion, a dialogue that seeks understanding and unity.

2. This dialogue—through the Joint International Commission—has proved fruitful and has made substantial progress. A common sacramental conception of the Church has emerged, sustained and passed on in time by apostolic succession. In our Churches, the apostolic succession is fundamental to the sanctification and unity of the People of God. Considering that in every local Church the mystery of divine love is realized and that this is how the Church of Christ shows forth its active presence in each one of them, the Joint Commission has been able to declare that our Churches recognize one another as Sister Churches, responsible together for safeguarding the one Church of God, in fidelity to the divine plan, and in an altogether special way with regard to unity.

We thank the Lord of the Church from the bottom of our hearts because these affirmations we have made together not only hasten the way to solving the existing difficulties, but henceforth enable Catholics and Orthodox to give a common witness of faith.

3. This is particularly appropriate on the eve of the third millennium when, two thousand years after the birth of Christ, all Christians are preparing to make an examination of conscience on the reality of His proclamation of salvation in history and among men. We will celebrate this Great Jubilee on our pilgrimage toward full unity and toward that blessed day, which we pray is not far off, when we will be able to share the same bread and the same cup, in the one Eucharist of the Lord.

Let us invite our faithful to make this spiritual pilgrimage together toward the Jubilee. Reflection, prayer, dialogue, reciprocal forgiveness, and mutual fraternal love will bring us closer to the Lord and will help us better to understand His will for the Church and for humanity.

4. In this perspective we urge our faithful, Catholics and Orthodox, to reinforce the spirit of brotherhood which stems from the one Baptism and from participation in the sacramental life. In the course of history and in the more recent past, there have been attacks and acts of oppression on both sides. As we prepare, on this occasion, to ask the Lord for His great mercy, we invite all to forgive one another and to express a firm will that a new relationship of brotherhood and active collaboration will be established.

Such a spirit should encourage both Catholics and Orthodox, especially where they live side by side, to a more intense collaboration in the cultural, spiritual, pastoral, educational, and social fields, avoiding any temptation to undue zeal for their own community to the disadvantage of the other. May the good of Christ's Church always prevail! Mutual support and the exchange of gifts can only make pastoral activity itself more effective and our witness to the Gospel we desire to proclaim more transparent.

5. We maintain that a more active and concerted collaboration will also facilitate the Church's influence in promoting

peace and justice in situations of political or ethnic conflict. The Christian faith has unprecedented possibilities for solving humanity's tensions and enmity.

6. In meeting one another, the Pope of Rome and the Ecumenical Patriarch have prayed for the unity of all Christians. In their prayers, they have included all the baptized faithful, who are incorporated into Christ, and they have asked for an even deeper fidelity to His Gospel for the various communities.

7. They bear in their heart a concern for all humanity, without any discrimination according to race, color, language, ideology, or religion. Therefore, they encourage dialogue, not only between the Christian Churches, but also with the various religions, and above all, with those that are monotheistic.

All this doubtless represents a contribution and a presupposition for strengthening peace in the world, for which our Churches pray constantly. In this spirit, we declare, without hesitation, that we are in favor of harmony among peoples and their collaboration, especially in what concerns us most directly, we pray for the full realization of the European Union, without delay, and we hope that its borders will be extended to the East.

At the same time, we also make an appeal that everyone will make a determined effort to solve the current burning problem of ecology, in order to avoid the great risk threatening the world today due to abuse of resources that are God's gift.

May the Lord heal the wounds tormenting humanity today and hear our prayers and those of our faithful for peace in our Churches and in all the world.

— 2 —

A Code of
Environmental Ethics

Pope John Paul II and
Ecumenical Patriarch Bartholomew

THE VATICAN AND VENICE, JUNE 10, 2002

We are gathered here today in the spirit of peace for the good of all human beings and for the care of creation.

At this moment in history, at the beginning of the third millennium, we are saddened to see the daily suffering of a great number of people from violence, starvation, poverty, and disease.

This Common Declaration was signed jointly via satellite connection between the Vatican and Venice, where Ecumenical Patriarch Bartholomew chaired the closing session of the Fourth International Symposium on religion, science, and environment, which assembled over two hundred scientists and theologians, as well as leaders and journalists from Greece to Italy, with stops in Albania, Montenegro, Bosnia-Herzegovina, Croatia, and Slovenia to explore threatened regions of the Adriatic Sea.

We are also concerned about the negative consequences for humanity and for all creation resulting from the degradation of some basic natural resources such as water, air, and land, brought about by an economic and technological progress which does not recognize and take into account its limits. Almighty God envisioned a world of beauty and harmony, and He created it, making every part an expression of His freedom, wisdom, and love (see Gn 1.1–25).

At the center of the whole of creation, He placed us, human beings, with our inalienable human dignity. Although we share many features with the rest of the living beings, Almighty God went further with us and gave us an immortal soul, the source of self-awareness and freedom, endowments that make us in His image and likeness (see Gn 1.26–31; 2.7). Marked with that resemblance, we have been placed by God in the world in order to cooperate with Him in realizing more and more fully the divine purpose for creation. At the beginning of history, man and woman sinned by disobeying God and rejecting His design for creation. Among the results of this first sin was the destruction of the original harmony of creation.

If we examine carefully the social and environmental crisis which the world community is facing, we must conclude that we are still betraying the mandate God has given us: to be stewards called to collaborate with God in watching over creation in holiness and wisdom. God has not abandoned the world. It is His will that His design and our hope for it will be realized through our cooperation in restoring its original harmony. In our own time we are witnessing a growth of ecological awareness which needs to be encouraged, so that it will lead to practical programs and initiatives. An awareness of the relationship between God and humankind brings a fuller sense of the importance of the relationship between human beings and the natural environment, which is God's creation and which God entrusted to us to guard with wisdom and love (see Gn 1.28).

Respect for creation stems from respect for human life and dignity. It is on the basis of our recognition that the world is created by God that we can discern an objective moral order within which to articulate a code of environmental ethics. In this perspective, Christians and all other believers have a specific role to play in proclaiming moral values and in educating people in ecological awareness, which is none other than responsibility toward self, toward others, toward creation.

What is required is an act of repentance on our part and a renewed attempt to view ourselves, one another, and the world around us within the perspective of the divine design for creation. The problem is not simply economic and technological; it is moral and spiritual. A solution at the economic and technological level can be found only if we undergo, in the most radical way, an inner change of heart, which can lead to a change in lifestyle and of unsustainable patterns of consumption and production.

A genuine conversion in Christ will enable us to change the way we think and act.

First, we must regain humility and recognize the limits of our powers and, most important, the limits of our knowledge and judgment. We have been making decisions, taking actions, and assigning values that are leading us away from the world as it should be, away from the design of God for creation, away from all that is essential for a healthy planet and a healthy commonwealth of people. A new approach and a new culture are needed, based on the centrality of the human person within creation and inspired by environmentally ethical behavior stemming from our triple relationship to God, to self, and to creation. Such an ethics fosters interdependence and stresses the principles of universal solidarity, social justice, and responsibility, in order to promote a true culture of life.

Second, we must frankly admit that humankind is entitled to something better than what we see around us. We and, much more, our children and future generations are entitled to a better world, a world free from degradation, violence, and bloodshed, a world of generosity and love.

Third, aware of the value of prayer, we must implore God the Creator to enlighten people everywhere regarding the duty to respect and carefully guard creation.

We therefore invite all men and women of goodwill to ponder the importance of the following ethical goals:

1. To think of the world's children when we reflect on and evaluate our options for action.
2. To be open to study the true values based on the natural law that sustain every human culture.
3. To use science and technology in a full and constructive way while recognizing that the findings of science have always to be evaluated in the light of the centrality of the human person, of the common good, and of the inner purpose of creation. Science may help us to correct the mistakes of the past, in order to enhance the spiritual and material well-being of the present and future generations. It is love for our children which will show us the path that we must follow into the future.
4. To be humble regarding the idea of ownership and to be open to the demands of solidarity. Our mortality and our weakness of judgment together warn us not to take irreversible actions with what we choose to regard as our property during our brief stay on this earth. We have not been entrusted with unlimited power over creation; we are only stewards of a common heritage.
5. To acknowledge the diversity of situations and responsibilities in the work for a better world environment. We do not expect every person and every institution to assume the same burden. Everyone has a part to play, but for the demands of justice and charity to be respected the most affluent societies must carry the greater burden, and from them is demanded a sacrifice greater than can be offered by the

poor. Religions, governments, and institutions are faced by many different situations; but on the basis of the principle of subsidiarity all of them can take on some tasks, some part of the shared effort.

6. To promote a peaceful approach to disagreement about how to live on this earth, about how to share it and use it, about what to change and what to leave unchanged. It is not our desire to evade controversy about the environment, for we trust in the capacity of human reason and the path of dialogue to reach agreement.

We commit ourselves to respect the views of all who disagree with us, seeking solutions through open exchange, without resorting to oppression and domination. It is not too late. God's world has incredible healing powers. Within a single generation, we could steer the earth toward our children's future. Let that generation start now, with God's help and blessing.

3

Dialogue of Charity

Pope John Paul II and
Ecumenical Patriarch Bartholomew

THE VATICAN, JUNE 29, 2004

Be watchful, stand firm in your faith, be courageous,
be strong. Let all that you do be done in love.
                                          —1 Corinthians 16.13–14

1. In the spirit of faith in Christ and the reciprocal love that unites us, we thank God for this gift of our new meeting that is taking place on the Feast of the Holy Apostles Peter and Paul and witnesses to our firm determination to continue on our way toward full communion with one another in Christ.

The Ecumenical Patriarch personally visited the Church of Rome to renew his commitment to dialogue between the two churches.

2. Many positive steps have marked our common journey, starting above all with the historical event that we are recalling today: the embrace of Pope Paul VI and Patriarch Athenagoras I on the Mount of Olives in Jerusalem, on January 5 and 6, 1964. We, their Successors, are meeting today to commemorate fittingly before God that blessed encounter, now part of the history of the Church, faithfully recalling it and its original intentions.

3. The embrace in Jerusalem of our respective predecessors of venerable memory visibly expressed a hope that dwells in all hearts, as the Communiqué declared: "With eyes turned to Christ, together with the Father, the Archetype and Author of unity and of peace, they pray God that this encounter may be the sign and prelude of things to come for the glory of God and the enlightenment of His faithful people. After so many centuries of silence, they have now met with the desire to do the Lord's will and to proclaim the ancient truth of His Gospel, entrusted to the Church."[1]

4. Unity and Peace! The hope kindled by that historic encounter has lit up our journey in these last decades. Aware that the Christian world has suffered the tragedy of separation for centuries, our predecessors and we ourselves have persevered in the "dialogue of charity," our gaze turned to that blessed, shining day on which it will be possible to communicate with the same cup of the precious Blood and the holy Body of the Lord.[2] The many ecclesial events that have punctuated these past years have put on firm foundations the commitment to brotherly love: a love which, in learning from past lessons, may be ready to forgive, more inclined to believe in good than in evil, and intent first and foremost on complying with the Divine Redeemer and in being attracted and transformed by Him.[3]

5. Let us thank the Lord for the exemplary gestures of reciprocal love, participation, and sharing that He has granted us to make; among them, it is only right to recall the pope's visit to Ecumenical Patriarch Demetrios in 1979, when the creation of

the Joint International Commission for Theological Dialogue between the Catholic Church and all the Orthodox Churches was announced at the Phanar, a further step to sustain the "dialogue of truth" with the "dialogue of charity"; Patriarch Demetrios's visit to Rome in 1987; our meeting in Rome on the Feast of Sts. Peter and Paul in 1995, when we prayed in St Peter's, despite the painful separation during the celebration of the Eucharistic Liturgy, since we cannot yet drink from the same chalice of the Lord. Then, more recently, there was the meeting at Assisi for the "Day of Prayer for Peace in the World," and the "Common Declaration on Environmental Ethics for the Safeguard of Creation," signed on June 10, 2002 [in the context of the Fourth Symposium on Ecology: The Adriatic Sea: A Sea at Risk—Unity of Purpose].

6. Despite our firm determination to journey on toward full communion, it would have been unrealistic not to expect obstacles of various kinds: doctrinal, first of all, but also the result of conditioning by a troubled history. In addition, the new problems which have emerged from the radical changes that have occurred in political and social structures have not failed to make themselves felt in relations between the Christian Churches. With the return to freedom of Christians in Central and Eastern Europe, old fears have also been reawakened, making dialogue difficult. Nonetheless, St. Paul's exhortation to the Corinthians, let all things be done in charity, must always be vibrant within us and between us.

7. The Joint International Commission for Theological Dialogue between the Catholic Church and all the Orthodox Churches, created with so much hope, has marked our progress in recent years. It is still a suitable instrument for studying the ecclesiological and historical problems that are at the root of our difficulties, and for identifying hypothetical solutions to them. It is our duty to persevere in the important commitment to reopen the work as soon as possible. In examining the reciprocal initiatives of the offices of Rome and of Constantinople with this in

view, we ask the Lord to sustain our determination and to convince everyone of how essential it is to pursue the "dialogue of truth."

8. Our meeting in Rome today also enables us to face certain problems and misunderstandings that have recently surfaced. The long experience of the "dialogue of charity" comes to our aid precisely in these circumstances, so that difficulties can be faced serenely without slowing or clouding our progress on the journey we have undertaken toward full communion in Christ.

9. Before a world that is suffering every kind of division and imbalance, today's encounter is intended as a practical and forceful reminder of the importance for Christians and for the Churches to coexist in peace and harmony, in order to witness in agreement to the message of the Gospel in the most credible and convincing way possible.

10. In the special context of Europe, moving in the direction of higher forms of integration and expansion toward the east of the continent, we thank the Lord for this positive development and express the hope that in this new situation, collaboration between Catholics and Orthodox may grow. There are so many challenges to face together in order to contribute to the good of society: to heal with love the scourge of terrorism; to instill a hope of peace; to help set aright the multitude of grievous conflicts; to restore to the European continent the awareness of its Christian roots; to build true dialogue with Islam, since indifference and reciprocal ignorance can only give rise to diffidence and even hatred; to nourish an awareness of the sacred nature of human life; to work to ensure that science does not deny the divine spark that every human being receives with the gift of life; to collaborate so that our earth may not be disfigured and that creation may preserve the beauty with which it has been endowed by God; but above all, to proclaim the Gospel message with fresh vigor, showing contemporary men and women how the Gospel

can help them to rediscover themselves and to build a more humane world.

11. Let us pray to the Lord to give peace to the Church and to the world, and to imbue our journey toward full communion with the wisdom of His Spirit, *ut unum in Christo simus* [so that we may be one in Christ].

4

Dialogue of Truth

Pope Benedict XVI and
Ecumenical Patriarch Bartholomew

THE PHANAR, NOVEMBER 30, 2006

This is the day that the Lord has made, let us rejoice and be glad in it.

—Psalm 117.24

This fraternal encounter which brings us together, Pope Benedict XVI of Rome and Ecumenical Patriarch Bartholomew of Constantinople–New Rome, is God's work, and in a certain sense His

On the occasion of the visit of Pope Benedict to Istanbul after his election on April 19, 2005, this Common Declaration marked the restoration of the official theological dialogue between the two churches that had suspended its regular sessions ten years earlier.

gift. We give thanks to the Author of all that is good, who allows us once again, in prayer and in dialogue, to express the joy we feel as brothers and to renew our commitment to move toward full communion. This commitment comes from the Lord's will and from our responsibility as Pastors in the Church of Christ. May our meeting be a sign and an encouragement for us to share the same sentiments and the same attitudes of fraternity, cooperation, and communion in charity and truth. The Holy Spirit will help us to prepare the great day of the reestablishment of full unity, whenever and however God wills it. Then we shall truly be able to rejoice and be glad.

1. We have recalled with thankfulness the meetings of our venerable predecessors, blessed by the Lord, who showed the world the urgent need for unity and traced sure paths for attaining it, through dialogue, prayer, and the daily life of the Church. Pope Paul VI and Patriarch Athenagoras I went as pilgrims to Jerusalem, to the very place where Jesus Christ died and rose again for the salvation of the world, and they also met again, here in the Phanar and in Rome. They left us a common declaration which retains all its value; it emphasizes that true dialogue in charity must sustain and inspire all relations between individuals and between Churches, that it "must be rooted in a total fidelity to the one Lord Jesus Christ and in mutual respect for their own traditions" (*Tomos Agapis*, 195). Nor have we forgotten the reciprocal visits of His Holiness Pope John Paul II and His Holiness Demetrios I. It was during the visit of Pope John Paul II, his first ecumenical visit, that the creation of the Joint Commission for Theological Dialogue between the Roman Catholic Church and the Orthodox Church was announced. This Commission brought our Churches together with the declared aim of reestablishing full communion.

As far as relations between the Church of Rome and the Church of Constantinople are concerned, we cannot fail to recall the solemn ecclesial act effacing the memory of the ancient anathemas which for centuries have had a negative effect on relations between our Churches. We have not yet drawn from this act all the positive consequences which can flow from it in our progress toward full unity, to which the Joint Commission is called to make an important contribution. We exhort our faithful to take an active part in this process, through prayer and through significant gestures.

2. At the time of the plenary session of the Joint Commission for Theological Dialogue, which was recently held in Belgrade through the generous hospitality of the Serbian Orthodox Church, we expressed our profound joy at the resumption of the theological dialogue. This had been interrupted for several years because of various difficulties, but now the commission has been able to work afresh in a spirit of friendship and cooperation. In treating the topic "Conciliarity and Authority in the Church" at the local, regional, and universal levels, the commission undertook a phase of study on the ecclesiological and canonical consequences of the sacramental nature of the Church. This will permit us to address some of the principal questions that are still unresolved. We are committed to offer unceasing support, as in the past, to the work entrusted to this commission, and we accompany its members with our prayers.

3. As pastors, we have first of all reflected on the mission to proclaim the Gospel in today's world. This mission, "Go, make disciples of all nations" (Mt 28.19), is today more timely and necessary than ever, even in traditionally Christian countries. Moreover, we cannot ignore the increase of secularization, relativism, even nihilism, especially in the Western world. All this calls for a renewed and powerful proclamation of the Gospel, adapted to the cultures of our time. Our traditions represent for us a patrimony which must be continually shared, proposed, and interpreted anew. This is why we must strengthen our cooperation and our common witness before the world.

4. We have viewed positively the process that has led to the formation of the European Union. Those engaged in this great project should not fail to take into consideration all aspects

affecting the inalienable rights of the human person, especially religious freedom, a witness and guarantor of respect for all other freedoms. In every step toward unification, minorities must be protected, with their cultural traditions and the distinguishing features of their religion. In Europe, while remaining open to other religions and to their cultural contributions, we must unite our efforts to preserve Christian roots, traditions, and values, to ensure respect for history, and thus to contribute to the European culture of the future and to the quality of human relations at every level. In this context, how could we not evoke the very ancient witnesses and the illustrious Christian heritage of the land in which our meeting is taking place, beginning with what the Acts of the Apostles tells us in evoking the figure of St. Paul, apostle to the gentiles? In this land, the Gospel message and the cultural tradition of the ancient world met. This link, which has contributed so much to the Christian heritage that we share, remains timely and will bear more fruit in the future for evangelization and for our unity.

5. Our concern extends to those parts of today's world where Christians live and to the difficulties they have to face, particularly poverty, wars, and terrorism but equally to various forms of exploitation of the poor, of migrants, of women and children. We are called to work together to promote respect for the rights of every human being, created in the image and likeness of God, and to foster economic, social, and cultural development. Our theological and ethical traditions can offer a solid basis for a united approach in preaching and action. Above all, we wish to affirm that killing innocent people in God's name is an offense against Him and against human dignity. We must all commit ourselves to the renewed service of humanity and the defense of human life, every human life.

We take profoundly to heart the cause of peace in the Middle East, where our Lord lived, suffered, died, and rose again, and where a great multitude of our Christian brethren have lived for centuries. We fervently hope that peace will be reestablished in that region, that respectful coexistence will be strengthened between the different peoples who live there, between the Churches, and between the different religions found there. To this end, we encourage the establishment of closer relationships between Christians, and of an authentic and honest interreligious dialogue, with a view to combating every form of violence and discrimination.

6. At present, in the face of the great threats to the natural environment, we want to express our concern at the negative consequences for humanity and for the whole of creation which can result from economic and technological progress that does not know its limits. As religious leaders, we consider it one of our duties to encourage and to support all efforts made to protect God's creation and to bequeath to future generations a world in which they will be able to live.

7. Finally, our thoughts turn toward all of you, the faithful of our Churches throughout the world, bishops, priests, deacons, men and women religious, lay men and women engaged in ecclesial service, and all the baptized. In Christ we greet other Christians, assuring them of our prayers and our openness to dialogue and cooperation. In the words of the apostle to the gentiles, we greet all of you: "Grace to you and peace from God our Father and the Lord Jesus Christ" (2 Cor 1.2).

— 5 —

Anniversary
of a Milestone

*Pope Francis and
Ecumenical Patriarch Bartholomew*

1. Like our venerable predecessors Pope Paul VI and Ecumenical Patriarch Athenagoras who met here in Jerusalem fifty years ago, we too, Pope Francis and Ecumenical Patriarch Bartholomew, were determined to meet in the Holy Land "where our common Redeemer, Christ our Lord, lived, taught, died, rose again, and

Issued on the occasion of the joint Apostolic Pilgrimage to the Holy Land by Pope Francis and Ecumenical Patriarch Bartholomew to mark the fiftieth anniversary since the visit to Jerusalem by Pope Paul VI and Ecumenical Patriarch Athenagoras in 1964.

ascended into Heaven, whence he sent the Holy Spirit on the infant Church."[1] Our meeting, another encounter of the Bishops of the Churches of Rome and Constantinople founded respectively by the two brothers, the apostles Peter and Andrew, is a source of profound spiritual joy for us. It presents a providential occasion to reflect on the depth and the authenticity of our existing bonds, themselves the fruit of a grace-filled journey on which the Lord has guided us since that blessed day of fifty years ago.

2. Our fraternal encounter today is a new and necessary step on the journey toward the unity to which only the Holy Spirit can lead us, that of communion in legitimate diversity. We call to mind with profound gratitude the steps that the Lord has already enabled us to undertake. The embrace exchanged between Pope Paul VI and Patriarch Athenagoras here in Jerusalem, after many centuries of silence, paved the way for a momentous gesture, the removal from the memory and from the midst of the Church of the acts of mutual excommunication in 1054. This was followed by an exchange of visits between the respective Sees of Rome and Constantinople, by regular correspondence and, later, by the decision announced by Pope John Paul II and Patriarch Demetrios, of blessed memory both, to initiate a theological dialogue of truth between Catholics and Orthodox. Over these years, God, the source of all peace and love, has taught us to regard one another as members of the same Christian family, under one Lord and Savior, Jesus Christ, and to love one another, so that we may confess our faith in the same Gospel of Christ, as received by the apostles and expressed and transmitted to us by the Ecumenical Councils and the Church Fathers. While fully aware of not having reached the goal of full communion, today we confirm our commitment to continue walking together toward the unity for which Christ our Lord prayed to the Father so "that all may be one" (Jn 17.21).

3. Well aware that unity is manifested in love of God and love of neighbor, we look forward in eager anticipation to the day in which we will finally partake together in the eucharistic ban-

quet. As Christians, we are called to prepare to receive this gift of eucharistic communion, according to the teaching of St. Irenaeus of Lyon,[2] through the confession of the one faith, persevering prayer, inner conversion, renewal of life, and fraternal dialogue. By achieving this hoped for goal, we will manifest to the world the love of God by which we are recognized as true disciples of Jesus Christ (see Jn 13.35).

4. To this end, the theological dialogue undertaken by the Joint International Commission offers a fundamental contribution to the search for full communion among Catholics and Orthodox. Throughout the subsequent times of Popes John Paul II and Benedict XVI and Patriarch Demetrios, the progress of our theological encounters has been substantial. Today we express heartfelt appreciation for the achievements to date, as well as for the current endeavors. This is no mere theoretical exercise but an exercise in truth and love that demands an ever deeper knowledge of each other's traditions in order to understand them and to learn from them. Thus we affirm once again that the theological dialogue does not seek a theological lowest common denominator on which to reach a compromise but is rather about deepening one's grasp of the whole truth that Christ has given to His Church, a truth that we never cease to understand better as we follow the Holy Spirit's promptings. Hence, we affirm together that our faithfulness to the Lord demands fraternal encounter and true dialogue. Such a common pursuit does not lead us away from the truth; rather, through an exchange of gifts, through the guidance of the Holy Spirit, it will lead us into all truth (see Jn 16.13).

5. Yet even as we make this journey toward full communion we already have the duty to offer common witness to the love of God for all people by working together in the service of humanity, especially in defending the dignity of the human person at every stage of life and the sanctity of family based on marriage, in promoting peace and the common good, and in responding to the suffering that continues to afflict our world. We acknowledge

that hunger, poverty, illiteracy, and the inequitable distribution of resources must constantly be addressed. It is our duty to seek to build together a just and humane society in which no one feels excluded or marginalized.

6. It is our profound conviction that the future of the human family depends also on how we safeguard—both prudently and compassionately, with justice and fairness—the gift of creation that our Creator has entrusted to us. Therefore, we acknowledge in repentance the wrongful mistreatment of our planet, which is tantamount to sin before the eyes of God. We reaffirm our responsibility and obligation to foster a sense of humility and moderation so that all may feel the need to respect creation and to safeguard it with care. Together we pledge our commitment to raising awareness about the stewardship of creation; we appeal to all people of goodwill to consider ways of living less wastefully and more frugally, manifesting less greed and more generosity for the protection of God's world and the benefit of His people.

7. There is likewise an urgent need for effective and committed cooperation of Christians in order to safeguard everywhere the right to express publicly one's faith and to be treated fairly when promoting that which Christianity continues to offer to contemporary society and culture. In this regard, we invite all Christians to promote an authentic dialogue with Judaism, Islam, and other religious traditions. Indifference and mutual ignorance can only lead to mistrust and unfortunately even conflict.

8. From this holy city of Jerusalem, we express our shared profound concern for the situation of Christians in the Middle East and for their right to remain full citizens of their homelands. In trust we turn to the almighty and merciful God in a prayer for peace in the Holy Land and in the Middle East in general. We especially pray for the Churches in Egypt, Syria, and Iraq, which have suffered most grievously due to recent events. We encourage all parties regardless of their religious convictions to continue to work for reconciliation and for the just recognition of people's rights. We are persuaded that it is not arms but dialogue, pardon,

and reconciliation that are the only possible means to achieve peace.

9. In a historical context marked by violence, indifference, and egoism, many men and women today feel that they have lost their bearings. It is precisely through our common witness to the good news of the Gospel that we may be able to help the people of our time to rediscover the way that leads to truth, justice, and peace. United in our intentions, and recalling the example, fifty years ago here in Jerusalem, of Pope Paul VI and Patriarch Athenagoras, we call upon all Christians, together with believers of every religious tradition and all people of goodwill, to recognize the urgency of the hour that compels us to seek the reconciliation and unity of the human family while fully respecting legitimate differences for the good of all humanity and of future generations.

10. In undertaking this shared pilgrimage to the site where our one same Lord Jesus Christ was crucified, buried, and rose again, we humbly commend to the intercession of the Most Holy and Ever Virgin Mary our future steps on the path toward the fullness of unity, entrusting to God's infinite love the entire human family. "May the Lord let His face shine upon you, and be gracious to you! The Lord look upon you kindly and give you peace!" (Nm 6.25–26).

— 6 —

Confirmation of Common Witness

Pope Francis and
Ecumenical Patriarch Bartholomew

THE PHANAR, NOVEMBER 30, 2014

We, Pope Francis and Ecumenical Patriarch Bartholomew, express our profound gratitude to God for the gift of this new encounter enabling us, in the presence of the members of the Holy Synod, the clergy, and the faithful of the Ecumenical Patriarchate, to celebrate together the feast of St. Andrew, the first-called and brother of the apostle Peter. Our remembrance of the apostles, who proclaimed the good news of the Gospel to the world through their preaching and their witness of martyrdom,

Joint statement during the official visit by Pope Francis to the Ecumenical Patriarchate.

31

strengthens in us the aspiration to continue to walk together in order to overcome, in love and in truth, the obstacles that divide us.

On the occasion of our meeting in Jerusalem last May, in which we remembered the historical embrace of our venerable predecessors Pope Paul VI and Ecumenical Patriarch Athenagoras, we signed a joint declaration. Today on the happy occasion of this further fraternal encounter, we wish to reaffirm together our shared intentions and concerns.

We express our sincere and firm resolution, in obedience to the will of our Lord Jesus Christ, to intensify our efforts to promote the full unity of all Christians, and above all between Catholics and Orthodox. As well, we intend to support the theological dialogue promoted by the Joint International Commission, instituted exactly thirty-five years ago by Ecumenical Patriarch Demetrios and Pope John Paul II here at the Phanar, which is currently dealing with the most difficult questions that have marked the history of our division and that require careful and detailed study. To this end, we offer the assurance of our fervent prayer as Pastors of the Church, asking our faithful to join us in praying "that all may be one, that the world may believe" (Jn 17.21).

We express our common concern for the current situation in Iraq, Syria, and the whole Middle East. We are united in the desire for peace and stability and in the will to promote the resolution of conflicts through dialogue and reconciliation. While recognizing the efforts already being made to offer assistance to the region, at the same time we call on all those who bear responsibility for the destiny of peoples to deepen their commitment to suffering communities and to enable them, including the Christian ones, to remain in their native land. We cannot resign ourselves to a Middle East without Christians, who have professed the name of Jesus there for two thousand years. Many of our brothers and sisters are being persecuted and have been forced violently from their homes. It even seems that the value of human life has been lost, that the human person no longer matters and may be sacrificed to other interests. And, tragically, all this is met by the indifference of many. As St. Paul reminds us, "If one member suffers, all suffer together; if one member is honored, all rejoice together" (1 Cor 12.26). This is the law of the Christian life, and in this sense we can say that there is also an ecumenism of suffering. Just as the blood of the martyrs was a seed of strength and fertility for the Church, so too the sharing of daily sufferings can become an effective instrument of unity. The terrible situation of Christians and all those who are suffering in the Middle East calls not only for our constant prayer but also for an appropriate response on the part of the international community.

The grave challenges facing the world in the present situation require the solidarity of all people of goodwill, so we also recognize the importance of promoting a constructive dialogue with Islam based on mutual respect and friendship. Inspired by common values and strengthened by genuine fraternal sentiments, Muslims and Christians are called to work together for the sake of justice, peace, and respect for the dignity and rights of every person, especially in those regions where they once lived for centuries in peaceful coexistence and now tragically suffer together the horrors of war. Moreover, as Christian leaders, we call on all religious leaders to pursue and to strengthen interreligious dialogue and to make every effort to build a culture of peace and solidarity between persons and between peoples. We also remember all the people who experience the sufferings of war. In particular, we pray for peace in Ukraine, a country of ancient Christian tradition, while we call upon all parties involved to pursue the path of dialogue and of respect for international law in order to bring an end to the conflict and allow all Ukrainians to live in harmony.

Our thoughts turn to all the faithful of our Churches throughout the world, whom we greet, entrusting them to Christ our Savior, that they may be untiring witnesses to the love of God. We raise our fervent prayer that the Lord may grant the gift of peace in love and unity to the entire human family.

"May the Lord of peace Himself give you peace at all times and in every way. The Lord be with all of you" (2 Thes 3.16).

Ecumenical Patriarch Bartholomew and Pope John Paul II. Photo courtesy of
Nikolaos Manginas.

Pope Benedict XVI and Ecumenical Patriarch Bartholomew embrace after signing the joint statement "Dialogue of Truth" at the Phanar in 2006. Photo courtesy of Greek American News Photo Agency, Dimitrios S. Panagos.

Pope Benedict XVI and Ecumenical Patriarch Bartholomew at the Phanar in 2006. Photo courtesy of Greek American News Photo Agency, Dimitrios S. Panagos.

Pope Benedict XVI and Ecumenical Patriarch Bartholomew at the Phanar in 2006. Photo courtesy of Nikolaos Manginas.

Pope Benedict XVI and Ecumenical Patriarch Bartholomew at an interreligious conference in Naples in 2007. Photo courtesy of Nikolaos Manginas.

Pope Francis and Ecumenical Patriarch Bartholomew at the Vatican in 2013. Photo courtesy of Nikolaos Manginas.

Justin Welby, the Archbishop of Canterbury, and Ecumenical Patriarch Bartholomew at the Phanar in 2014. Photo courtesy of Nikolaos Manginas.

Pope Francis and Ecumenical Patriarch Bartholomew meet in Jerusalem in 2014. Photo courtesy of Greek American News Photo Agency, Dimitrios S. Panagos.

Pope Francis and Ecumenical Patriarch Bartholomew at the Church of the Holy Sepulcher in 2014. Photo courtesy of Nikolaos Manginas.

Pope Francis and Ecumenical Patriarch Bartholomew sign the joint statement "Anniversary of a Milestone" in Jerusalem in 2014. Photo courtesy of Nikolaos Manginas.

Pope Francis and Ecumenical Patriarch Bartholomew embrace after signing the joint statement "Anniversary of a Milestone." Photo courtesy of Nikolaos Manginas.

Pope Francis and Ecumenical Patriarch Bartholomew at the Patriarchal Church of St. George in 2014. Photo courtesy of John Mindala.

Pope Francis and Ecumenical Patriarch Bartholomew sign the joint statement "Confirmation of Common Witness" at the Phanar in 2014. Photo courtesy of Nikolaos Manginas.

Pope Francis and Ecumenical Patriarch Bartholomew at the Divine Liturgy for the feast day of Saint Andrew the Apostle in 2014. Photo courtesy of John Mindala.

Ecumenical Patriarch Bartholomew, Pope Francis, and Archbishop Ieronymos signing the joint statement "Responding to the Refugee Crisis" in Lesbos in 2016. Photo courtesy of Nikolaos Manginas.

Justin Welby, the Archbishop of Canterbury, and Ecumenical Patriarch Bartholomew sign the joint statement "Standing up to Modern Slavery" at the Phanar in 2017. Photo courtesy of Nikolaos Manginas.

Rev. John I. Jenkins, C.S.C., and Ecumenical Patriarch Bartholomew at the University of Notre Dame in 2021. Photo by Matt Cashore/University of Notre Dame.

— 7 —

Climate Change
and Human Health

*Ecumenical Patriarch Bartholomew
and Justin Welby, Archbishop of Canterbury*

THE PHANAR AND CANTERBURY,
JUNE 19, 2015

On June 23, the *Lancet* medical journal and University College
London will publish a landmark report, highlighting the inalienable and undeniable link between climate change and human
health. We warmly welcome the report's message of hope, which
confirms the fact that climate change is more than just a technological or financial challenge and confirms the voice of health in
the discussion on climate change. Indeed, the central premise of

Joint statement published in the *New York Times* in light of a report by the Lancet
Commission and in anticipation of the Paris Agreement.

35

the Commission's work is that tackling climate change could be the single greatest health opportunity of the twenty-first century.

It is no surprise that climate change has the potential to dismantle decades of health developments while also threatening the well-being of future generations through the ongoing detrimental impact on air and water, as well as food security and nutrition. Those with little or no access to healthcare—both children and the elderly in particular—are more vulnerable to such predicaments.

However, health is symptomatic of a larger problem, which undermines and fragments our broader worldview. In addition to highlighting the effects of climate change, we must address the root of the problem. In so doing, we will discover how the benefits of assuming moral responsibility and taking immediate action—not just on matters related to health, but also economy and policy—far outweigh the cost of remaining indifferent and passive.

It is this vital link that the Lancet Commission's Report on Health and Climate Change conclusively and authoritatively demonstrates. In short, it proves that our response to climate change—in terms of both mitigation and adaptation—will reduce human suffering while preserving the diversity and beauty of God's creation for our children. God's generous and plentiful creation, which we so often take for granted, is a free gift to all living creatures and all living things. We must, therefore, ensure that the resources of our planet are—and continue to be—enough for all to live abundant lives.

The report could not appear at a more significant and sensitive time in history. This year, as all eyes look ahead to the Paris climate negotiations and as governments prepare to sign a universal commitment to limit global temperature rises, we have reached a critical turning point. We are now—like never before—in a position to choose charity over greed and frugality over wastefulness in order to affirm our moral commitment to our neighbor and our respect toward the earth. Basic human rights—

such as access to safe water, clean air, and sufficient food—should be available to everyone without distinction or discrimination.

Our faith is in God as Creator, Redeemer, and Sustainer. Our mission is from Christ's invitation to discern the presence of God in—and do justice by—human beings and created nature. Our obligation is to work together for a better world, one in which all human beings can flourish; our Christian vocation is to proclaim the Gospel inclusively and comprehensively.

To this purpose, as early as the mid-1980s, when creation care was neither political nor fashionable, the Ecumenical Patriarchate initiated pioneering environmental initiatives. In 1989 it established a day of prayer for the protection of the natural environment and from 1991 to this day instigated a series of symposia and summits on an international, interfaith, and interdisciplinary basis. Its ecumenical and ecological vision has been embraced in parishes and communities throughout the world.

In 1984 the Anglican Consultative Council adopted the Five Marks of Mission. The fifth of these is "To strive to safeguard the integrity of creation, and sustain and renew the life of the earth." In 2006 the Church of England launched its national environment campaign, Shrinking the Footprint, to enable the whole Church to address—in faith, practice, and mission—the issue of climate change. In 2015 a clear direction has been set for the Church of England's National Investing Bodies in support of the transition to a low carbon economy that brings its investments into line with the Church's witness.

As representatives of two major Christian communions, we appeal to the world's governments to act decisively and conscientiously by signing an ambitious and hopeful agreement in Paris during COP [UN Conference of the Parties] 21 at the end of this year. We hope and pray that this covenant will contain a clear and convincing long-term goal that will chart the course of decarbonization in the coming years. Only in this way can we reduce the inequality that flows directly from climate injustice within and between countries.

The Lancet Report is further proof that all of us must act with generosity and compassion toward our fellow human beings by acting on climate change now. This is a shared moral responsibility and urgent requirement. Civil society, governmental authorities, and religious leaders have an opportunity to make a difference in a way that bridges our diverse opinions and nationalities.

— 8 —

Responding to the Refugee Crisis

Pope Francis,
Ecumenical Patriarch Bartholomew,
and Archbishop Ieronymos
of Athens and All Greece

LESVOS, GREECE, APRIL 16, 2016

We, Pope Francis, Ecumenical Patriarch Bartholomew, and Archbishop Ieronymos of Athens and All Greece, have met on the Greek island of Lesvos to demonstrate our profound concern

Joint Declaration initiated by Ecumenical Patriarch Bartholomew with Pope Francis and Archbishop Ieronymos of Athens and All Greece on the occasion of their common visit to the refugee camp of Moria on the Greek island of Lesvos.

for the tragic situation of the numerous refugees, migrants, and asylum seekers who have come to Europe fleeing from situations of conflict and, in many cases, daily threats to their survival. World opinion cannot ignore the colossal humanitarian crisis created by the spread of violence and armed conflict, the persecution and displacement of religious and ethnic minorities, and the uprooting of families from their homes, in violation of their human dignity and their fundamental human rights and freedoms.

The tragedy of forced migration and displacement affects millions and is fundamentally a crisis of humanity, calling for a response of solidarity, compassion, and generosity and an immediate practical commitment of resources. From Lesvos, we appeal to the international community to respond with courage in facing this massive humanitarian crisis and its underlying causes, through diplomatic, political, and charitable initiatives and through cooperative efforts, both in the Middle East and in Europe.

As leaders of our respective Churches, we are one in our desire for peace and in our readiness to promote the resolution of conflicts through dialogue and reconciliation. While acknowledging the efforts already being made to provide help and care to refugees, migrants, and asylum seekers, we call upon all political leaders to employ every means to ensure that individuals and communities, including Christians, remain in their homelands and enjoy the fundamental right to live in peace and security. A broader international consensus and an assistance program are urgently needed to uphold the rule of law, to defend fundamental human rights in this unsustainable situation, to protect minorities, to combat human trafficking and smuggling, to eliminate unsafe routes, such as those through the Aegean and the entire Mediterranean, and to develop safe resettlement procedures. In this way we will be able to assist those countries directly engaged in meeting the needs of so many of our suffering brothers and sisters. In particular, we express our solidarity with the people of Greece, who despite their own economic difficulties have responded with generosity to this crisis.

Together we solemnly plead for an end to war and violence in the Middle East, a just and lasting peace, and the honorable return of those forced to abandon their homes. We ask that religious communities increase their efforts to receive, assist, and protect refugees of all faiths and that religious and civil relief services work to coordinate their initiatives. For as long as the need exists, we urge all countries to extend temporary asylum, to offer refugee status to those who are eligible, to expand their relief efforts, and to work with all men and women of goodwill for a prompt end to the conflicts in course.

Europe today faces one of its most serious humanitarian crises since the end of the Second World War. To meet this grave challenge, we appeal to all followers of Christ to be mindful of the Lord's words, on which we will one day be judged: "For I was hungry and you gave me food; I was thirsty and you gave me drink; I was a stranger and you took me in; I was naked and you clothed me; I was sick and you visited me; I was in prison and you came to me. . . . Assuredly, I say to you, inasmuch as you did it to one of the least of these my brethren, you did it to me" (Mt 25.35–36, 40).

For our part, in obedience to the will of our Lord Jesus Christ, we firmly and wholeheartedly resolve to intensify our efforts to promote the full unity of all Christians. We reaffirm our conviction that "reconciliation [among Christians] involves promoting social justice within and among all peoples. . . . Together we will do our part toward giving migrants, refugees, and asylum seekers a humane reception in Europe" (*Charta Oecumenica*, 2001). By defending the fundamental human rights of refugees, asylum seekers, and migrants, and the many marginalized people in our societies, we aim to fulfill the Churches' mission of service to the world.

Our meeting today is meant to help bring courage and hope to those seeking refuge and to all those who welcome and assist them. We urge the international community to make the protection of human lives a priority and, at every level, to support inclusive policies which extend to all religious communities. The terrible situation of all those affected by the present humanitarian crisis, including so many of our Christian brothers and sisters, calls for our constant prayer.

9

Standing up to Modern Slavery

Ecumenical Patriarch Bartholomew
and Justin Welby, Archbishop of Canterbury

THE PHANAR, FEBRUARY 7, 2017

1. We, Bartholomew, Archbishop of Constantinople–New Rome and Ecumenical Patriarch, and Justin Welby, Archbishop of Canterbury and Primate of All England, cosponsored a special international Forum on Modern Slavery titled "Sins Before Our Eyes" at the Phanar on February 6–7, 2017. The forum, originally proposed during the official visit by the Ecumenical Patriarch to Lambeth Palace in November 2015, was a high-level gathering of distinguished scholars, practitioners, and policy makers from

Joint statement at the inaugural Forum on Modern Slavery cosponsored by the Ecumenical Patriarch and the Archbishop of Canterbury.

around the world who were invited to discuss the contemporary problem of human exploitation. The Forum also takes place in the context of "2017: The Year of the Sanctity of Childhood," as declared by the Ecumenical Patriarchate.

2. For religious communities worldwide and for the global human rights community, the protection of human dignity and fundamental human rights is of utmost importance. The role of the Church in the world is "to preach good news to the poor, to bind up the brokenhearted, to proclaim release to the captives and to set at liberty the oppressed" (Is 61.1; Lk 4.18). This was clearly articulated in the final Encyclical of the Holy and Great Council of the Orthodox Church (Crete, June 2016): "The Church lives not for herself. She offers herself for the whole of humanity in order to raise up and renew the world into a new heaven and a new earth."

3. We are convinced that there is an intimate and inseparable link between preserving God's natural creation and protecting God's image in every human being, especially those most vulnerable to the myriad forms of human exploitation that comprise the sin of modern slavery. The same arrogance and greed are to blame for the oppression and exploitation of innocent victims—most often children and women—of human trafficking, human smuggling, prostitution, the sale of human organs, indentured labor, and the many other dimensions of modern slavery. Each and every person bears the burden and pays the price for the fact that there are more people in slavery today than at any other time in history.

4. In his keynote address, the Ecumenical Patriarch observed, "The Orthodox Church is often accused of neglecting the world for the sake of liturgical worship and spiritual life, turning primarily toward the Kingdom of God to come, disregarding challenges of the present. In fact, however, whatever the Church says, whatever the Church does, is done in the Name of God and for the sake of human dignity and the eternal destiny of

the human being. It is impossible for the Church to close its eyes to evil, to be indifferent to the cry of the needy, oppressed and exploited. True faith is a source of permanent struggle against the powers of inhumanity." In his opening address, Archbishop Welby emphasized, "Slavery is all around us, but we are too blind to see it. It is in our hands, and yet we are too insensitive to touch it. The enslaved are next to us in the streets, but we are too ignorant to walk alongside them. It must not be relegated to a footnote in history. It is still a living reality in all of our communities, as I have seen from personal experience in the United Kingdom, not because we think it is acceptable, but because our sin lies in blindness and ignorance."

5. Therefore,

(i) We condemn all forms of human enslavement as the most heinous of sins, inasmuch as it violates the free will and the integrity of every human being created in the image of God.

(ii) We commend the efforts of the international community and endorse the United Nations Protocol to Prevent, Suppress and Punish Trafficking in Persons, especially Women and Children.

(iii) We pray that all victims of modern slavery may be liberated in order to rebuild their lives and that the perpetrators may be brought to justice.

(iv) We repent for not doing nearly enough swiftly enough to curb the plague of modern slavery, acknowledging that our ignorance and indifference are the worst forms of tolerance and complicity. We are judged each day by what we refuse to see and fail to do for the most vulnerable among us.

(v) We appeal to local and national governments to pass and implement strict laws against modern slavery, with a budget and capability to ensure organizations are held to account for modern slavery in their supply chains while also allocating resources and services for trafficking victims, who are exposed to and endangered by such injustice.

(vi) We encourage our leaders to find appropriate and effective ways of prosecuting those involved in human trafficking, preventing all forms of modern slavery, and protecting its victims in our communities and promoting hope wherever people are exploited.

(vii) We urge our faithful and communities—the members of the Orthodox Church and the Church of England—as well as all people of goodwill to become educated, raise awareness, and take action with regard to these tragedies of modern slavery and to commit themselves to working and praying actively toward the eradication of this scourge against humanity.

(viii) We commit to the establishment of a joint task force for modern slavery to bring forward timely recommendations as to how the Orthodox Church and the Church of England can collaborate in the battle against this cruel exploitation.

10

World Day of Prayer for Creation

*Pope Francis and
Ecumenical Patriarch Bartholomew*

THE VATICAN AND THE PHANAR,
SEPTEMBER 1, 2017

The story of creation presents us with a panoramic view of the world. Scripture reveals that, "in the beginning," God intended humanity to cooperate in the preservation and protection of the natural environment. At first, as we read in Genesis, "no plant of the field was yet in the earth and no herb of the field had yet sprung up—for the Lord God had not caused it to rain upon the

The first joint encyclical by Ecumenical Patriarch Bartholomew and Pope Francis, published on September 1, 2017, marking the World Day of Prayer for Creation.

earth, and there was no one to till the ground" (Gn 2.5). The earth was entrusted to us as a sublime gift and legacy, for which all of us share responsibility until, "in the end," all things in heaven and on earth will be restored in Christ (see Eph 1.10). Our human dignity and welfare are deeply connected to our care for the whole of creation.

However, "in the meantime," the history of the world presents a very different context. It reveals a morally decaying scenario where our attitude and behavior toward creation obscures our calling as God's co-operators. Our propensity to interrupt the world's delicate and balanced ecosystems, our insatiable desire to manipulate and control the planet's limited resources, and our greed for limitless profit in markets—all these have alienated us from the original purpose of creation. We no longer respect nature as a shared gift; instead, we regard it as a private possession. We no longer associate with nature in order to sustain it; instead, we lord over it to support our own constructs.

The consequences of this alternative worldview are tragic and lasting. The human environment and the natural environment are deteriorating together, and this deterioration of the planet weighs upon the most vulnerable of its people. The impact of climate change affects, first and foremost, those who live in poverty in every corner of the globe. Our obligation to use the earth's goods responsibly implies the recognition of and respect for all people and all living creatures. The urgent call and the challenge to care for creation are an invitation for all of humanity to work toward sustainable and integral development.

Therefore, united by the same concern for God's creation and acknowledging the earth as a shared good, we fervently invite all people of goodwill to dedicate a time of prayer for the environment on September 1. On this occasion, we wish to offer thanks to the loving Creator for the noble gift of creation and to pledge commitment to its care and preservation for the sake of future generations. After all, we know that we labor in vain if the Lord is not by our side (see Ps 126–27), if prayer is not at the center of our reflection and celebration. Indeed, an objective of our prayer is to change the way we perceive the world in order to change the way we relate to the world. The goal of our promise is to be courageous in embracing greater simplicity and solidarity in our lives.

We urgently appeal to those in positions of social and economic, as well as political and cultural, responsibility to hear the cry of the earth and to attend to the needs of the marginalized but above all to respond to the plea of millions and support the consensus of the world for the healing of our wounded creation. We are convinced that there can be no sincere and enduring resolution to the challenge of the ecological crisis and climate change unless the response is concerted and collective, unless the responsibility is shared and accountable, unless we give priority to solidarity and service.

A Universal Appeal for a Global Challenge

Pope Francis,
Ecumenical Patriarch Bartholomew,
and Justin Welby, Archbishop of Canterbury

THE VATICAN, THE PHANAR,
AND LAMBETH PALACE,
SEPTEMBER 1, 2021

For more than a year, we have all experienced the devastating effects of a global pandemic—all of us, whether poor or wealthy, weak or strong. Some were more protected or vulnerable than others, but the rapidly spreading virus meant that we have de-

The first joint statement by the three global leaders, initiated by Ecumenical Patriarch Bartholomew, in light of the twenty-sixth United Nations climate change conference in Glasgow.

pended on each other in our efforts to stay safe. We realized that, in facing this worldwide calamity, no one is safe until everyone is safe, that our actions really do affect one another, and that what we do today affects what happens tomorrow.

These are not new lessons, but we have had to face them anew. May we not waste this moment. We must decide what kind of world we want to leave to future generations. God mandates, "Choose life, so that you and your children might live" (Dt 30.19). We must choose to live differently; we must choose life.

September is celebrated by many Christians as the Season of Creation, an opportunity to pray and care for God's creation. As world leaders prepare to meet in November at Glasgow to deliberate on the future of our planet, we pray for them and consider the choices we must all make. Accordingly, as leaders of our Churches, we call on everyone, whatever their belief or worldview, to endeavor to listen to the cry of the earth and of people who are poor, examining their behavior and pledging meaningful sacrifices for the sake of the earth which God has given us.

THE IMPORTANCE OF
SUSTAINABILITY

In our common Christian tradition, the Scriptures and the Saints provide illuminating perspectives for comprehending both the realities of the present and the promise of something larger than what we see in the moment. The concept of stewardship— of individual and collective responsibility for our God-given endowment—presents a vital starting point for social, economic, and environmental sustainability. In the New Testament, we read of the rich and foolish man who stores a great wealth of grain while forgetting about his finite end (Lk 12.13–21). We learn of the prodigal son who takes his inheritance early, only to squander it and end up hungry (Lk 15.11–32). We are cautioned against adopting short-term and seemingly inexpensive options of building on sand, instead of building on rock for our common home to withstand storms (Mt 7.24–27). These stories invite us to adopt a broader outlook and recognize our place in the extended story of humanity.

But we have taken the opposite direction. We have maximized our own interest at the expense of future generations. By concentrating on our wealth, we find that long-term assets, including the bounty of nature, are depleted for short-term advantage. Technology has unfolded new possibilities for progress but also for accumulating unrestrained wealth, and many of us behave in ways which demonstrate little concern for other people or the limits of the planet. Nature is resilient, yet delicate. We are already witnessing the consequences of our refusal to protect and preserve it (Gn 2.15). Now, in this moment, we have an opportunity to repent, to turn around in resolve, to head in the opposite direction. We must pursue generosity and fairness in the ways that we live, work, and use money, instead of selfish gain.

THE IMPACT ON PEOPLE LIVING WITH POVERTY

The current climate crisis speaks volumes about who we are and how we view and treat God's creation. We stand before a harsh justice: biodiversity loss, environmental degradation, and climate change are the inevitable consequences of our actions, since we have greedily consumed more of the earth's resources than the planet can endure. But we also face a profound injustice: the people bearing the most catastrophic consequences of these abuses are the poorest on the planet and have been the least responsible for causing them. We serve a God of justice, who delights in creation and creates every person in God's image but also hears the cry of people who are poor. Accordingly, there is an innate call within us to respond with anguish when we see such devastating injustice.

Today we are paying the price. The extreme weather and natural disasters of recent months reveal afresh to us with great force and at great human cost that climate change is not only a future challenge, but an immediate and urgent matter of survival. Widespread floods, fires, and droughts threaten entire continents. Sea levels rise, forcing whole communities to relocate; cyclones devastate entire regions, ruining lives and livelihoods. Water has become scarce and food supplies have become insecure, causing conflict and displacement for millions of people. We have already seen this in places where people rely on small-scale agricultural holdings. Today we see it in more industrialized countries where even sophisticated infrastructure cannot completely prevent extraordinary destruction.

Tomorrow could be worse. Today's children and teenagers will face catastrophic consequences unless we take responsibility now, as "fellow workers with God" (Gn 2.4–7), to sustain our world. We frequently hear from young people who understand that their futures are under threat. For their sake, we must choose to eat, travel, spend, invest, and live differently, thinking not only of immediate interest and gains but also of future benefits. We repent of our generation's sins. We stand alongside our younger sisters and brothers throughout the world in committed prayer and dedicated action for a future which corresponds ever more to the promises of God.

THE IMPERATIVE
OF COOPERATION

Over the course of the pandemic, we have learned how vulnerable we are. Our social systems frayed, and we found that we cannot control everything. We must acknowledge that the ways we use money and organize our societies have not benefited everyone. We find ourselves weak and anxious, submersed in a series of crises: health, environmental, food, economic, and social, which are all deeply interconnected.

These crises present us with a choice. We are in a unique position either to address them with shortsightedness and profiteering or seize this as an opportunity for conversion and transformation. If we think of humanity as a family and work together toward a future based on the common good, we could find ourselves living in a very different world. Together we can share a vision for life where everyone flourishes. Together we can choose to act with love, justice, and mercy. Together we can walk toward a fairer and fulfilling society with those who are most vulnerable at the center.

But this involves making changes. Each of us, individually, must take responsibility for the ways we use our resources. This path requires an ever closer collaboration among all Churches in their commitment to care for creation. Together, as communities, churches, cities, and nations, we must change route and discover new ways of working together to break down the traditional barriers between peoples, to stop competing for resources and start collaborating.

To those with more far-reaching responsibilities—heading administrations, running companies, employing people, or investing funds—we say: choose people-centered profits; make short-term sacrifices to safeguard all our futures; become leaders in the transition to just and sustainable economies. "To whom much is given, much is required" (Lk 12.48).

This is the first time that the three of us feel compelled to address together the urgency of environmental sustainability, its impact on persistent poverty, and the importance of global cooperation. Together, on behalf of our communities, we appeal to the heart and mind of every Christian, every believer, and every person of goodwill. We pray for our leaders who will gather in Glasgow to decide the future of our planet and its people. Again, we recall Scripture: "Choose life, so that you and your children may live" (Dt 30.19). Choosing life means making sacrifices and exercising self-restraint.

All of us—whoever and wherever we are—can play a part in changing our collective response to the unprecedented threat of climate change and environmental degradation.

Caring for God's creation is a spiritual commission requiring a response of commitment. This is a critical moment. Our children's future and the future of our common home depend on it.

NOTES

INTRODUCTION

1. "The Phanar" is the traditional way of denoting the seat of the Ecumenical Patriarchate, based on the lantern or lighthouse (Greek *phanari*) that was a unique characteristic of the Istanbul region.

2. Oliver Clément, *Conversations* (Crestwood, NY: St. Vladimir's Seminary Press, 1997); John Chryssavgis, *Bartholomew* (New York: HarperCollins, 2016).

3. Ecumenical Patriarch Bartholomew, *Encountering the Mystery: Understanding Orthodox Christianity Today* (New York: Doubleday Books, 2008); Ecumenical Patriarch Bartholomew, *In the World, Yet Not of the World: Social and Global Initiatives of Ecumenical Patriarch Bartholomew*, ed. John Chryssavgis (New York: Fordham University Press, 2010); Ecumenical Patriarch Bartholomew, *Speaking the Truth in Love: Theological and Spiritual Exhortations of Ecumenical Patriarch Bartholomew*, ed. John Chryssavgis (New York: Fordham University Press, 2011); and Ecumenical Patriarch Bartholomew, *On Earth as in Heaven: Ecological Vision and Initiatives of Ecumenical Patriarch Bartholomew*, ed. John Chryssavgis (New York: Fordham University Press, 2012).

4. Dimitri Obolensky, *The Byzantine Commonwealth: Eastern Europe, 500–1453* (London: Weidenfeld and Nicolson), 1971.

5. Ecumenical Patriarch Bartholomew, *Encountering the Mystery*, 19.

6. See Athanasios Papas [former Metropolitan of Chalcedon], "Restoration of Churches, Monasteries and Pilgrimages in the Archdiocese of Constantinople and Its Neighboring Metropolitan Sees," *Kleronomia* 36 (2004): 1–2 [in Greek]; reprinted, Thessalonika: Patriarchal Institute of Patristic Studies (2007), 223–48.

7. John Chryssavgis, *Cosmic Grace, Humble Prayer: The Ecological Vision of the Green Patriarch Bartholomew*, rev. ed. (Grand Rapids, MI: Eerdmans, 2009), 256–61.

8. Address to the Archaeological Society of Athens, "The Ecumenical Conscience of the Church of Constantinople and the Concern for all Churches," *Ekklesia* (1987): 5–29 [in Greek].

9. Phanariote bishops are those presiding in areas geographically close to the Phanar. On the *endemousa synodos*, see Joseph Hajjar, *Le Synode Permanent (Synodos Endemousa) dans l'Eglise Byzantine des origins au XIe siècle* (Rome: Orientalia Christiana Analecta, 1962).

10. For the formal process of recognition or reception of saints, see the 1931 "Report of the Synodal Committee of the Ecumenical Patriarchate for Canonical Affairs on the Proclamation of Saints in the Orthodox Church," in Georgios Tsetsis, *The Incorporation of Saints in the Calendar of Feasts* (Katerini: Tertios Publications, 1991), 167–71 [in Greek].

11. *Epistle* 120, PG 54.1407.

12. In the official publication of the Orthodox Church in America (OCA), *The Orthodox Church* 14, no. 4 (1978): 4.

13. See John Chryssavgis, ed., *Speaking the Truth in Love: Theological and Spiritual Exhortations of Ecumenical Patriarch Bartholomew* (New York: Fordham University Press, 2011), 119–21.

14. In May 2001 Pope John Paul II issued a similar apology during an official visit to Greece. See www.irishtimes.com/news/greek-press -hails-pope-s-historic-apology-1.382843.

15. See www.lastampa.it/2015/06/18/vaticaninsider/metropoli tan-zizioulas-laudato-si-is-an-occasion-of-great-joy-and-satisfaction -for-the-orthodox-9OC5q2xdD2pJqXY3ArkqzI/pagina.html.

16. For the full text, see www.vatican.va/content/francesco/en /encyclicals/documents/papa-francesco_20201003_enciclica-fratelli -tutti.html.

17. For the full text, see www.goarch.org/social-ethos.

18. The two documents cover many similar topics. *Fratelli Tutti* discusses racism and immigration, interfaith relations and international politics, as well as care for the poor and underprivileged, "liberty, equality, and fraternity," women and war, capital punishment and private property, economy and equity. *For the Life of the World* discusses the role of the church in the public square, the course of human life from conception to death, wealth and poverty, civil and social justice, violence and war, as well as the struggle for peace and reconciliation, ecumenical relations and interreligious tolerance, human rights and religious freedom, and science and technology.

19. The only other similar document in the Orthodox Church was produced by the Patriarchate of Moscow in 2000, just as Orthodox Christians there began to evaluate their place in a post-Soviet world.

20. As of today, the document has gained international attention: eminent journals have devoted special issues to it, seminars and webinars have been organized, and two monographs have already appeared. The Vatican Dicastery for Promoting Integral Human Development is considering a joint Roman Catholic–Orthodox Christian project to draft common ethical principles and goals.

CLIMATE CHANGE

1. David Bentley Hart and John Chryssavgis, eds., *For the Life of the World: Toward a Social Ethos of the Orthodox Church* (Brookline, MA: Holy Cross Orthodox Press, 2020), 103.

JOINT STATEMENTS

1. In the case of the Ecumenical Patriarchate, the feast is conventionally called "thronal," a reference to the continuity of the Throne of Constantinople.

2. See Will Cohen, *The Concept of "Sister Churches" in Catholic-Orthodox Relations since Vatican II* (Muenster: Aschendorff Verlag), esp. ch. 2, 48–69.

3. This was the first of three occasions (1995, 2004, and 2008) that Bartholomew—or any ecumenical patriarch—has attended Feast of Saints Peter and Paul at the Vatican. Popes John Paul II, Benedict XVI, and Francis have each attended the Feast of St. Andrew at the Phanar on one occasion (1979, 2006, and 2014 respectively).

4. For the two statements (by Pope Paul VI and Ecumenical Patriarch Athenagoras), see *Tomos Agapis: Vatican–Phanar 1958–1970* (Rome and Istanbul, 1971), 285–89, 290–94. For an English translation, see E. J. Stormon, *Towards the Healing of Schism: The Sees of Rome and Constantinople* (New York: Paulist Press, 1987), 130–31.

5. See *Tomos Agapis*, 444–47; see also Stormon, *Towards the Healing of Schism*, 181–82.

6. See Stormon, *Towards the Healing of Schism*, 367–68.

3 — DIALOGUE OF CHARITY

1. *Common Declaration of Pope Paul VI and Patriarch Athenagoras I, Tomos Agapis* (Vatican-Phanar, 1971), 120 n. 50.

2. Address of Patriarch Athenagoras I to Pope Paul VI [January 5, 1964], in *Common Declaration*, 109 n. 48.

3. Address of Pope Paul VI to Patriarch Athenagoras I [January 6, 1964], in *Common Declaration*, 117 n. 49.

5 — ANNIVERSARY OF A MILESTONE

1. Common communiqué of Pope Paul VI and Patriarch Athenagoras, published after their meeting of January 6, 1964.

2. *Against Heresies* IV.18.5; PG 7.1028.

ECUMENICAL PATRIARCH BARTHOLOMEW
is the 270th archbishop of Constantinople.
He is the spiritual leader of
Eastern Orthodox Christians worldwide.

JOHN CHRYSSAVGIS
is the author of numerous books and a theologian
serving as archdeacon of the Ecumenical Patriarchate
and advisor to the ecumenical patriarch
on theological and environmental issues.

Printed in the USA
CPSIA information can be obtained
at www.ICGtesting.com
LVHW061955101023
760704LV00001B/1